PREPARE TO WORK UNTIL YOU DIE

MAKE PASSIVE INCOME

ARVIND UPADHYAY

The goal of passive income is to earn money while you sleep. This is how to get your assets working for you. You invest time in building something upfront that will generate income down the road with little effort on your part.

Building a business that requires time upfront but allows you to work less as the business gets going is a great way to generate passive income.

Investing in financial products that produce dividend income or interest income and appreciate in value over time is ideal.

There are many ways a beginner can start investing and making money. As Warren Buffet is known to say, "If you don't find a way to make money while you sleep, you will work until you die."

Often when people need more money they turn to a part time job or side hustle. The better option would be to stop trading time for money and create passive income.Starting an online business and becoming financially independent is now a realistic proposition for anyone who has a computer and internet access. Of the many different ways to go about doing this, some will provide a good return for your efforts, but unfortunately, many online businesses just do not succeed and people operating them fail to earn enough to make it worthwhile. There are many instances where someone has written an eBook and published it, or opened an online retail store, only to find there are no buyers The only way to make money anywhere is to have paying customers; the trick is how to get them. There are a few good ways to get customers or traffic to your website and this book is about successful proven strategies that you can use to build a long term passive income from the internet. Some of the things that worked a few years ago are no longer viable because the internet is always changing, growing and evolving. With 3.5 billion existing customers using the net daily and another 3 billion potential customers in Africa, India, China and the rest of Asia, the sky is the limit for new businesses and an unlimited income source. Now is the perfect time to catch the so called "gravy train", but you need traffic, quality content and to be prepared to do the necessary work (often quite a lot of work). But just doing the work is no guarantee of success; you have to be working in the right areas and doing the right things Living from a "passive income" as it is called, is a term now used to describe the income people receive from the internet. It is called passive income because in theory most of the work is pre done and then you sit back and reap the benefits of your labor with little work involved. In practice, any online business will require ongoing maintenance, the amount needed depends on the site, it's application and the product you are supplying. There are many different styles of internet businesses ranging from those that require a daily input to some that are totally automated. Some internet businesses are realistic and practical ways to earn money on the net. Many people have written some sort of original intellectual property, such as an eBook, an online course, blog posts or similar, then set up an online store to promote their product. Whether they are made or created by the operator, or acquired from other sources, there is a considerable amount of time and energy needed to set up the site and customize it. Once all this is done and your site has gone live, you will then need to perform various marketing tasks such as promoting your site or posts and interacting with people on social media. Finding similar sites or blogs and giving quality feedback and comments is a great way to promote your own site as long as it is done in a positive way. A good blog or website has fresh quality content added on a regular basis to encourage people to keep coming back, not just preloaded with content and left to stagnate. Much of the material in a blog or website can come from someone else you hire to write the post for you, but you're the one who has to edit them, schedule them, and oversee the whole operation. All of these things are not passive at all and the profits, if any, can be very allusive if you are not careful. There are hundreds of get rich schemes that pop up all the time. They usually follow the same pattern or similar rag to riches "Cinderella Story", where this person was on the verge of bankruptcy or committing suicide because they were so desperate. Then, because of the love of their family or their dog, they decided to give the internet just one last shot, or they stumbled across a person who, for whatever reason, gave them an instant formula to make fantastic amounts of money. Now they make a 6-figure income working less than 1 hour daily while sitting on their private beach in the middle of a private paradise that they paid for in cash after only 1 year of using this formula. Now they want to give back and are offering this information free to you if you part with...wait for it...not $1200, or $600... or even $100. It is yours today exclusively and only for specially selected people at today's spot price of $9.99, but hurry this offer is limited, (please do not trip over the huge pile of B-S). This or some similar such dribble will only make money for the person who is selling the scheme. If you want to take the time, and have the ability to create a fantasy similar to the one above, it is a reasonable way to make a passive income for a while, although you have to live with yourself knowing you are just ripping people off (usually desperate people who cannot afford it). There is no doubt that a few people will make an easy dollar on the internet, but most people will struggle at least at first, finding it hard to make the same as you would if you had a normal job. But if you are prepared to put in the time and energy needed it is a very good and sound way to provide a lasting long term income. Building a solid long term passive income on the internet requires several things; the most important is having traffic. Traffic is the term used to describe the people coming or visiting your website. it is a simple formula: the more people who visit your site, the more money you can make; no traffic, no money, full stop. It does not matter how good or how cheap your product or service offer is, if there is no one to see it then no one will buy it. The second very important thing is having something other people want and are willing to pay you to get it. The next important thing is your credibility on the net. This, like traffic, can take some time to build up, but there are several ways to speed it up. You can buy a mailing list off the internet with hundreds and sometimes thousands of email addresses, but these are usually of little value for several reasons. These lists are old and have been used by many people to try to sell their stuff so the response level is very low. The other reason these lists are of dubious value is because you are better to try and get quality leads of people who have expressed an interest in whatever you are offering rather than just firing emails that will end in most people's spam or junk mail files. If it even gets past their spam blockers. This book will explore different methods to making a long term passive income. It will advise you of some of their good and bad points, advantages and drawbacks, so you can make an informed decision on the best way for you to proceed.

other finacial books by Arvind Upadhyay

Game Of Investing Money Like The Rich

Books by Arvind Upadhyay

This Can Bring Riches to You

Books by Arvind Upadhyay

INSIGHT OF THE MONEY

Books by Arvind Upadhyay

think like a rich

Books by Arvind Upadhyay

how to be rich early in early 20s

Books by Arvind Upadhyay

Contents

Foreword

There are many ways a beginner can start investing and making money. As Warren Buffet is known to say, “If you don’t find a way to make money while you sleep, you will work until you die.”

Often when people need more money they turn to a part time job or side hustle. The better option would be to stop trading time for money and create passive income.A passive income, by definition, is where you do a certain amount of work to provide an asset that you can make a return on. Some people have real estate that they collect rentals on or buy cheap and sell at a higher profit, others invest their money in stocks or bonds and live off the proceeds. For some people that do not have the capital to make a large investment that will service a lifestyle they wish to have, they will need to use other options such as creating or writing eBooks. This can represent a large investment in time as many eBooks take months or years to write. This type of investment can pay off as the book has the potential to keep selling for many years. Usually the people who are successful at obtaining a long term passive income do so by careful planning and spreading their resources over as large an area as is practicable as this will lessen the chances of any losses and maximize the chances of gaining a better income from your profit base. The old saying ‘don’t keep all your eggs in one basket’ is very wise. Many investors have come undone because they over invested in only one area and were unable to absorb the losses they incurred. Spending above your total capacity or not taking into account the need to service and maintain your web presence as well as taking risks that do not payoff are recipes for disaster and should be avoided. But common sense and forethought can go a long way to preventing most problems.

CHAPTER ONE

Creating a Passive Income From a Small Budget.

Creating a passive income on the internet is a dream for most people, but it can become a reality for anyone who has a computer and internet connection. Whether you are just starting to get interested in working on the internet and wish to find a way to have a passive income, or if you have been struggling to make an income from it, there are a few things you should consider before jumping in the deep end of the internet pool. Some important questions you should consider to help you decide on your best approach are: Do you have a product or service you wish to sell? This can be a product you have created whether physical or intellectual. Do you already have some sort of presence on the internet, a website, blog or social media accounts? Do you have a budget? What is your internet experience? What will you have to learn to be successful? There are a few excellent ways to start generating a passive income without spending a lot of money, but although it is possible to run a business without spending anything, this approach would usually be a very long process and require a large amount of work. The best strategy is to establish a budget you can afford and work within that. The greater amount you have in your budget, within reason, the faster and easier it is to reach an income level that will support your lifestyle. But be aware there are many people on the net who work on the principle that it is easy to separate a fool and his money so beware! Getting a presence on the internet can be accomplished by starting on social media sites like Facebook, Google Plus, Twitter, LinkedIn, YouTube, Pinterest, and Instagram, as well as using some of the lesser known local social media sites. The problem with these sites is they are now becoming so crowded that the competition is difficult to cope with and it is easy for your endeavors to get lost in the tide of information presented. A few years ago these sites worked well. Now, with over 3.5 Billion people using the internet regularly, it takes a bit of knowhow to use them effectively. Being very selective and careful in where you place your investment dollars is the key to success. To begin, you will require a web site, which could be in the form of a standard web page or possibly a blog. There are many companies who provide platforms for you to launch and maintain your website and what you choose really depends on what you are selling, the service you are promoting and your budget. Web hosting sites like the free Google My Sites is a good option as it has the major advantage of being free, and it is easily picked up by the Google search engines. But it comes with limitations. Other sites like Bluehost and Wordpress are my preferred options. I like these sites because they are very user friendly and have a good help service including a chat where you can talk to a company technician who can help you with any problems you may encounter. The Bluehost package, for only a few dollars a month, allows you to have a free domain name such as (I will use my name for an example) www.RichardGadson.com, so you can have your own website. With that you can create up to 10 sub-domains, or web pages, where you can promote your products or services. If you re promoting a cookbook for example, (whether you are the author or just promoting another author's work) your sub-domain could be OrganicCookingwithRichardGadson.com. The domain also comes with several email accounts. These are very handy and can be tailored to suit any application such as Richard@RichardGadson.com or RichardsCookbook@RichardGadson.com. It is always a good idea to use your name in your website. This is because there is no doubt about who the site belongs to and people will associate your name quickly with a quality product. That is assuming you only have quality products. If you use inferior products and do not give value for time and money spent then you will have a very short future on the internet. If you have a product that you want to try, but without your name associated with it, you can still use one of your sub-domains or create a new one by just not including your name in the internet address for that page. For example, you may find a great selection of chef's knives and make an arrangement with the manufacturer or supplier to sell them, so you can use one of your free sub-domains to do this. Another option is you may wish to create another eBook such as a dessert cookbook, and that could be on a sub-domain page of your main site, but with its own stand-alone web presence, linked or unlinked to your main site. When you start or join Bluehost and Wordpress or any of the other web hosting companies, they provide full directions on how to set up your own internet website and business, along with a load of helpful advice, so this book will not go into these physical details. An almost totally passive internet income could be achieved by outsourcing all the necessary work and only overseeing the operation, but that still requires some input, so there is no such thing as a totally passive income site. Having stated that, it is possible, and very reasonable, to have an extremely low maintenance income site, especially if you use and learn some of the tools and methods available from your WordPress site where it is possible to build monetization into your WordPress site and increase the earning potential of your sites with minimal effort. To make the most of these sites, you will still need to do all the general day to day site upkeep tasks such as writing new posts, marketing, and site maintenance, but the money-making approach you take can be quite simple and require little work on your part once set up.

CHAPTER TWO

Creating a Passive Income With a Larger Budget.

When investing in any money making enterprise, always remember that everything is relative; the amount you can expect to earn is relative to the risk involved . A low risk usually means there is a low interest rate and a high interest rate often means there is a greatly increased risk of not only earning, but of also losing your investment. The best way to determine if something can be a worthwhile passive income stream is by comparing the likely return with the current risk-free rate of return on, say, government bonds. The 10-year government bank bond yield is at about 3%, so that any venture you try should have a substantially better return than this, otherwise you are wasting your efforts since you can earn 3% doing nothing. It should be noted that different countries' governments set different rates. For example, in the Philippines you can get a return after tax (the government withholds the tax) of at least 7% on government bonds, and these rates are guaranteed by the Philippine government. (Some would say this is a bit risky, but they have never defaulted and are a better risk than many European countries' governments and banks.) So I would suggest that if you will not make a return of substantially over 7% p.a. then leave it alone unless you are doing this for a hobby. Internet Share Market Investing Most of us have heard how some people make a vast fortune investing on the stock market, and indeed, you can make substantial financial gains investing in stocks and shares. There are some very common mistakes that first time investors have to be aware of before they try investing in stocks. If you have a few hundred dollars to spare and just want to see what happens, that's ok, but if you are serious about creating a nice passive income, it is a real learning curve like anything else. Don't just jump in headfirst, although the basics of investing are quite simple in theory, that is, buy low and sell high.

Most people do not, in practice, however, know what low and high really mean. What is high to someone who is selling is usually considered low (or low enough) to the buyer in any transaction, so that different conclusions can be drawn from the same information. Because of the relative nature of the market, it is important to take the time to study what stocks or shares are doing before jumping in. Before starting you should learn at least the basic metrics such as book value, divided yield, price earnings ratios and so forth. Understand how they are calculated, where their major weaknesses lie and where these metrics have generally been for any stock and its industry over time. When you start out it is very helpful to use virtual money in a stock simulator or with a demo account as this can help you to understand how things work and save a substantial sum of money to start with. When you first look at penny stocks they seem like a great idea. With as little as $100, you can get a lot more shares in penny stocks than you could if buying a blue chip stock that could cost $50 or more (some much more) for a share. Penny stock gives a good profit if it goes up by a dollar. But, unfortunately, what penny stocks offer in their profitability has to be measured against the volatility they have. They are called penny stocks for a reason; usually they are low quality companies that, more often than not, will not work out as a profitable deal, losing 50 cents on a penny stock could mean a 100% loss. Losing 50 cents on a $50 deal is not so bad and can usually be reclaimed later, given time. Getting solid information on penny stocks can also be difficult, making them a poor choice for an investor who is still learning as they are exceptionally vulnerable. Overall, it is a good idea to think about stocks in percentages and not whole dollar amounts. When you first start out or until you become experienced in dealing with stocks, it is best for most people to own and deal with quality stock as a long term proposition rather than trying to make a quick buck on low-quality companies, as most returns on penny stocks are a matter of luck. Do not be tempted to invest everything in one specific investment; usually it is not a good move. Any company, even the best ones, can have issues and see their stocks decline dramatically. This happened in the last financial crash. Especially when just starting out, it is a sound idea to buy only a handful of stocks so you are less likely to have a huge loss in the event of problems, and overall ups and downs should even out to show a reasonable profit. The lessons learned while doing this then become less costly, but still valuable. Be very careful about borrowing to invest as nothing is ever a sure bet. If you borrow for stocks it is called leveraging your money. This magnifies both the gains and the losses on a given investment. If you have $100 to invest and decide to borrow $50 to buy $150 of a certain stock and the stock rises 10%, you make $15, or a 15% return on your capital. But, on the other hand, if the stock declines 10%, you would lose $15, or a 15% loss, but what is important to understand is that if the stock goes up by 50%, you will make a 75% return which is great, but, if the stock declines 50%, you lose all the money you borrowed and more. So until you have experience it is wise not to borrow to invest. It is important to be aware that you could potentially lose all your investments over night, so it is vital to only use money you can afford to lose. If you start out with an initial investment and make a few gains, take a percentage from the profits and reinvest that. Then, by slowly building up your total investment you will be in a stronger position without risking too much. Investing should be viewed as a long-term business, whether you are a trader, or a buying and holding type investor. To stay in business, you need to have some cash reserves on the side for emergencies and opportunities. This cash will not earn any return, but having all your cash in the market is a risk that even professional investors won't take. If you do not have enough cash to invest and keep some for an emergency cash reserve, then you're not in a position financially where investing makes sense. Sound advice is hard to find and trying to guess the next big thing or fastest growing share price, hot tips, or working on rumors is not a sound business plan and can be full of dangers for first time investors. Remember, you are competing with professional firms that not only get information the second it becomes available, but have had years of experience and know how to properly analyze it quickly. If you're lucky, you will win a few, but if your luck runs out you could lose everything. The best policy for beginners is to stick with investments in companies you understand and have personal experience dealing with. You should not treat investing like playing the lotto. When you are personally buying stocks in the market, you are competing against large mutual funds and professional investors that do this full-time and with far more resources and in-depth information than the average person can obtain. When you first begin investing, it is best to start small and take the risks with money you are prepared to lose, as the market can be unforgiving to any mistakes. As you become more adept at evaluating stocks, you can start making bigger investments. Money Trading Foreign Exchange Forex Trading Forex trading is all about the speculation on the price of one country's currency against another. Being a Forex trader offers one of the most amazing potential lifestyles of any profession in the world, but it is also one of the riskiest. But if you are determined and disciplined, you can make it happen. The way it works is if you think the euro is going to rise against the U.S. dollar, you can buy the EURUSD currency pair low and then (hopefully) sell it at a higher price to make a profit. If you buy the euro against the dollar (EURUSD), and the U.S. dollar strengthens, you will then be in a losing position. So it's important to be aware of the risk involved in trading in Forex, and not only the reward. As a trader you can make a lot of money fast or lose a lot of money fast. The very important thing when dealing in the money market is to know exactly what you're doing and always know the exact dollar amount you have at risk before entering a trade and be TOTALLY OK with losing that amount of money, because any one trade could be a loser. Forex is the largest market in the world, with daily volumes exceeding $3 trillion per day. Anyone can open a trading account with as little as $250 at many retail brokers and begin trading the same day in most cases. Straight through order execution allows you to trade at the click of a mouse. It has an advantage over trading in shares in that there are fewer currency pairs to focus on and you can trade anywhere in the world with the only requirements being a laptop and internet connection. There is commissionfree trading with many retail market-makers and overall lower transaction costs than stocks and commodities. On top of all that, traders have equal opportunity to profit in rising or falling markets. All beginners should be aware that trading carries both the potential for reward and risk. Many people come into the markets thinking only about the reward and ignoring the risks involved and this is the fastest way to lose all of your trading account money. If you want to get started trading in the Forex market, get on the right track and study it first. There are a few good sites on the net that offer free courses and it's critical that you are aware of and accept the fact that you could lose on any given trade.

CHAPTER THREE

Beginning with Different Strategies and Ideas

Online Advertising Online advertising is one of the simplest ways to earn money on the internet. This is especially true if you have yet to earn your first passive online income. But although it's a simple concept, in practice it's not necessarily easy without you doing proper research and learning the best methods to suit your individual application. To make a good income with this type of advertising, it requires a lot of traffic through your site because of the small amount gained by each click or visitor. Some of the best ways to have online advertising on your site or blog are by using the following: AdSense With Google AdSense you can earn passive online income from your website by showing ads that are relevant to your site and its visitors. One of the great things about AdSense is that Google does most of the hard work for you; they find the advertisers, pick the ads, track the clicks, and even deposit the earnings straight to your bank account each and every month. No wonder that 65% of the top 200 websites that show ads use AdSense. Media.Net Media.net is very similar to AdSense. It is the Yahoo! Bing Network's answer to AdSense ads and is probably the second largest contextual advertising company in the world. They have an approval process that is a bit more extensive than Google AdSense and require a certain number of page views monthly to get an account with them, but once established they can provide an income stream that is very similar to AdSense. Chitika Chitika is similar to AdSense and Media.net; they are one of the popular alternative ad networks to AdSense and have a low minimum payout threshold. Especially if you have a blog with less traffic, Chitika is a premium ad network which will show quality relevant ads. If you have a high-quality blog, you can expect a great income from Chitika. Affiliate Marketing Affiliate internet marketing has been around almost as long as the internet and this is one of the best and easiest ways to earn some totally passive income. Affiliate marketing is fairly simple. You earn money online by promoting the products or services of another company for a commission that is paid on each sale you make. The normal approach is to partner up with affiliate programs and almost all major internet businesses and companies have affiliate marketing programs. Once you join and get their affiliate links, you can start promoting them everywhere, on all your web activities In order to build a steady and increasing long term consistent income stream from affiliate marketing, you need to have traffic and to be promoting products that give people good value. To entice people to buy those products, you need to have a webpage that attracts a large amount of people and build a trusting relationship with your audience. Build your own email subscriber list from people who visit your website using a service like AWeber to capture emails and respond to queries. You will then be able to create a list of people that trust you and want to hear about what you have to say and they will then be more inclined to except your affiliate product recommendations. Usually it is best to limit the types of products to those that are closely associated with the theme or topic of your website or blog, because if you have too many adverts people will soon become annoyed or distracted and switch off, much the same way we do when the ads come on out TV. Some of the good affiliate broker services are Google Adsense , Amazon Associates , ClickBank , Commission Junction, Flex Offers, etc. They all have thousands of different products in all types of ideas and niches, so you will be sure to find some quality products to choose from. Email Marketing To be successful with email marketing it is very necessary not to be seen as a scammer or to be swamping people with irrelevant junk mail. You will be sure to lose people quickly from your mailing list if you do. If done correctly and tastefully though, this can be a very successful method of marketing because you are sending to people who know you and are receptive to you and your niche, thereby increasing the chances of more purchases. Niche Websites Niche websites are a sound and successful way to make a good income if you have a specialty product or service. They can be dedicated to one subject or a part of a subject and they then become of interest to a select number of people, but people who are more likely to purchase because they are interested in the subject of your website. These types of websites or niche websites are much easier to advertise and are better for being picked up by search engines, delivering you directly to the right customers. Another way to make money from niche sites is to sell them by auction at websites like Flippa. There is no reason not to have a whole portfolio of niche sites; these could be of related subjects or totally different independent standalone subjects, all contributing to your passive income. When you look at most successful internet entrepreneurs, they own or develop multiple websites because with each site it increases the potential you have for making more and more earnings. Writing Free-Lance People who are good at writing or who enjoy writing articles, blogs, and short fictional stories or just like writing in general about almost any topic can often find there is a market for readymade, good quality content that they may be able to sell on sites like Upwork, eLance or Freelancer. Some popular sites like eHow, About.com, and Yahoo are looking for writers and by selling or even just contributing regularly to these sites it can help build up your reputation. This, in turn. will help you to negotiate for better and better rates as well as being able to compete for some of the higher paying freelance jobs. Many of these will pay $50 per hour or more. But if doing this type of work, it is vital to keep in contact with the people you contract for as they like to know what's going on and not to be kept in the dark because they often have deadlines to meet. This is especially important if you have a long term contract or a longer term project. By sending them regular updates you will build people's confidence in your abilities and asking questions insures you have a good understanding of the work required. If you ever have a job and are finding it hard to deliver the promised work or to finish your contract, contact the people you are working for as soon as possible and let them know. Business is business and common courtesy goes a long way. People need to be sure you can be relied on or they will not employ you again and can very easily destroy your reputation, so don't ever do anything that is going to hurt your reputation. Search Engine Optimization or SEO Those people who have a working knowledge about or anyone who takes the time to learn about SEO, which is how search engines or websites work, would find there is a huge demand for different types of articles that are written in a style that optimizes search engine words such as keywords, keyword synonyms, title tags, headers, bullets, etc. Promoting Clickbank products Clickbank is now probably the biggest digital products marketplace online. One of the measurers it uses is called 'gravity' to represent how well a product sells, based on how many sales have been made and how recent these sales were. Clickbank has an affiliate program where you can find a huge range of products. Once you join up you can promote any of your own or other people's products, as well as find people who will promote your products, so you can potentially get a huge following for your site. Promoting Amazon Products The Amazon affiliate program is a really good way to promote physical products, either your own or other people's, through a reliable, trustworthy, and well-known online store. Their commissions are fairly small, but because everyone knows Amazon they have a huge amount of traffic. You can earn a commission when you send someone to Amazon if they buy anything else on Amazon within 24 hours, whether they end up buying the product you promoted or not. So, for example, if you promoted a book and the person you sent to Amazon ended up buying something else you will get the commission for both. This can add up to a nice extra bonus. Promoting Commission Junction Products Commission Junction is one of the oldest and largest affiliate networks on the internet today. Most of their merchants are well established which can be an advantage if you're looking to promote bigger brands. They offer several options including pay per sale offers, pay per lead offers and other types of offers. Promoting DigiResults Products Online business and internet marketing products are the main things DigiResults focus on, but they also have other products ranging from health and fitness to travel. Vendors and affiliates get paid at the point of sale, and not a month or two later like most affiliate marketplaces, which makes them more attractive. Simple Virtual Assistant Jobs Although this is not strictly passive income as you have to put in a small amount of effort, these things are good because you get paid for doing (very) simple tasks online. Cashbacks This is a great way to get rewarded for purchasing or using products you plan to buy anyway. Cashback sites pay you when you click through them, go to retailers, and spend. There are well over 2,000 stores that offer cashbacks including Walmart, Target, Sears, Calvin Klein, and others. You can also get a $10 gift card after your first $25 worth of purchases. Sign up is free. Taking Surveys There are many free survey websites offering users the ability to get paid for taking surveys online. These sites should all be free and if you encounter a survey site where sign up is not free, simply avoid it. There are many good sites. Take a look at Global TestMarket, Mobrog or Toluna Survey Center. You will never get rich taking surveys, but it is an interesting way to spend a few idle minutes and pay for that odd coffee. Answering Questions There are so many people asking questions on line and if you're an expert in your field, you can generate income by answering these questions. JustAnswer.com is a company that allows you to join their team of experts and serve a customer base of more than 20 million people. Fightfox.com is a place for travel experts so check them out. They have great reviews and positive commentary pretty much everywhere. Writing Reviews There are many companies that will pay you for writing reviews of their products and services, especially if you have a well-established blog or other online presence that is in the same or a similar field. Target Your Own Advertisers There is no reason why you cannot target advertisers directly who have or are advertising products relevant to your content and offer them deals or an arrangement to sell your products and you to sell theirs. Selling eBooks If done the right way, selling eBooks can be quite a good passive income stream. Once you have published your book and it is there permanently, it will just keep on selling a few copies (or if you're lucky, lots of copies) for years to come. Because there are millions of books out there, it is often hard to break into this market and it does take time to write a good book and usually it will take a while for it to start selling and provide you with an income, but if you've got a lot of knowledge about a particular topic and love to write, the new technology makes it really easy for anyone to write, edit, and self-publish your own eBook for free. With little trouble you can make a very good income with eBooks. These can sell for as little as $0.99, all the way up to +$100, depending on the content and the demand for books of your chosen topic. One of the really great things about writing and self-publishing eBooks is that most of the online book stores such as Amazon, (who are by far the biggest) as well as almost all the others, will list and sell it for you with no upfront fees. You pay a commission on sales and they handle everything, including marketing sales and book distribution, then deposit the money into your account or send you a check. You are also free (as you own the book) to sell and market it in any other market place such as eBay, ClickBank, or through your own or friends' and associates' webpages or blogs. Selling Your eBook on Amazon If you are going to sell eBooks, then Amazon is the best choice because they are the biggest online eBook retailer and generate around three quarters of all eBook sales via their website. They will give you a return of 70% royalty on each book sold. The only problem is they do not disclose the email address of the purchaser so you cannot add them to your mailing list for updates and future sales . S ell Your eBook on Your Own Website Having your own website, and selling your own and other people's books and products can be very lucrative. You gain the attention of your customers and the ability to add them to your mailing list so that you can invite them to come back to your site so that you can offer them some more of your products or services. This is part of building up the all-important traffic, especially this type of traffic as these people have already come to you so they are much more likely to become repeat or regular customers; this is what's known as quality traffic. Online Courses If you can write an eBook there is no reason you cannot write or create an online course. This is another very good way to leverage your time and effort by teaching something once and getting paid for it over and over again. Many people feel that an online course or lessons are more valuable than eBooks, mainly because they can offer multimedia content such as video and audio and not just text. They usually also offer support, guidance or coaching as part of your course, which adds even more value. Chapter 3 : Selling Physical Products Online There is no reason that anyone needs to be limited to selling digital products. Selling or reselling physical products can be very lucrative. Making a living by purchasing wholesale and reselling on the existing online market places has never been easier. eBay eBay is now the biggest and most well-known auction and shopping site out on the net, with every country having its own local chapter as well as the main international site. The cost varies from country to country and usually you pay a small insertion fee to list your product and a small portion of the selling price (10%) when your item sells. Often, they run special promotion deals and at the moment, the insertion fees for your first 50 listings per calendar month are free. You can also open an eBay store if you wish to sell on a regular basis. There are some very good profits to be made by buying products that are cheap and advertised poorly or with restrictions that you could purchase and re promote attractively at a good markup. Re-Selling Other People's Stuff on eBay Sometimes you will find items where the people who listed them were not very careful about how they listed them, with no picture, terrible descriptions, no reserve, and other obstacles that have stopped people buying. These can become a real bargain for the smart investor. By buying these items at the right bargain price, and then advertising them properly with good photos and descriptions, it is possible to resell them at a substantial profit for almost no effort. Another good idea is to sell things on behalf of other people who, for whatever reason, do not want to sell it themselves. You just agree to take a mutually agreed upon commission. Checking out church fairs, garage sales, antique fairs, estate sales, opportunity shops, and auction houses, you can often find all manners of stuff being sold at a bargain price. These types of things can bring good sale on eBay (or any other similar site). After just a few easy sales, you could potentially double or quadruple your money. Drop Shipping Drop shipping is the ultimate passive income provider. It can be made to be totally automatic with your only input being to check the system and cash the checks. The term drop shipping is when you create an eStore front that offers products from certain manufacturers. The client visits your store, orders a product, or places an order with you, and someone else (usually an assembly company in another country, often India, or somewhere in South East Asia) makes the product inexpensively and ships it directly to the customer. You don't send the money to the manufacturer until after the client has paid you, so there is no risk involved, you never even see, handle, or do anything with the physical product other than manage the whole process (and even that can be outsourced if you really want). As a seller, this is incredibly efficient because you don't need to have any inventory, overhead costs, storage costs, and very little liability. So if you have a good idea for a product that could be mass-produced at an economical price, it could be original or something someone else provides, then drop shipping might be a great opportunity for you. Once you have a product, by using the drop ship method, you can sell anywhere, as well as in your own store, using companies like eBay or Amazon, or some of the other sites that are mentioned in this chapter to reach the widest audience possible. Take a look through Amazon at all the products available. The name brands are all there with their huge mark ups (you pay for the name, not necessarily the quality) and all the look-alike products are there as well. Many of them are poorly represented, so if your chosen product is presented properly, your SEO is in place, and you have priced it to compete, there is a lot of money to be made from the 3.5 billion people using the internet. Craigslist Craigslist does not offer the same features as eBay but it's free and many people find that it is easier and quicker to use. You do not have to join to become a member, although this is an option if you want to be able to keep track of your posts and repost your products. Etsy Etsy is a bit like eBay, but is focused on mostly handmade or vintage products. Perfect if you're selling anything artsy and crafty as they have an annual turnover in excess of 2 billion dollars and so are popular. Shopify Shopify is very simple and easy to set up. It provides options for you to build your own e-commerce store from scratch. It has an easy to use admin interface with over a hundred mobile responsive themes and loads of amazing add-on apps for all your e-commerce needs. Weebly Weebly is a simple and affordable way to build your own website as well as an online store or blog. You can pick your own or use one of their many themes, put your site together using a handy drag-and-drop creator, download the mobile app and start blogging and selling straight away. It is also a great site to use to manage your ad and promotion campaigns, manage social media channels and craft beautiful newsletters. Simplesite.com This site offers you a free website including a personal domain, unique designs, great customer service, as well as being mobile and tablet optimized, SEO optimized and comes with your own free online store. It's the perfect way to start an online passive income business on a shoe-string budget. Selling Other Digital Products There are many different types of digital products you can sell, in fact, anything you can think of has a potential market with 3.5 billion people on the net. Selling Websites and Domain Names Flippa.com is a great site for buying and selling websites and domain names and just like many things, including real estate, these can go up in value over time. Often, if you think of a great domain name and it is not taken, you can sell it. If someone wants that name it could be worth a lot and domain names sell from about $10 upwards, with some of the more popular ones fetching several thousand. In fact, sometimes an exceptionally good domain name can be worth many thousands of dollars. Think cocacola.com or gottahaveacoke.com. This would take a bit of time and knowhow but could produce a nice passive income over time. Sell Photos If you have a good camera and like taking photos, sites like Shutterstock, iStockphoto and Graphic Stock will accept all sorts of high-quality images and then sell them on their sites for a royalty fee. This can provide you with a good steady stream of passive income, as they all have hundreds of thousands of visitors daily. These are the sites many businesses use to easily and conveniently find the pictures they use for their websites and products. The music that you hear when the company you call is busy and you are put on hold, when listening to advertisements, or hear when watching a promotional video or something on you tube, often come from companies who sell stock music in the same way as they sell photos and other images. If you are musically inclined, there is money to be made by recording yourself. There is a steady demand as people search for fresh original talent and you do not have to be a professional to make money at this. For those of us who simply like photography or recording yourself or friends playing an instrument, don't let these images go to waste when you can easily license them through a royalty free website that specializes in stock photos or music. Each time someone uses something you have licensed you could receive a small commission or fee that, over time, could build into a nice little income stream to add to all the other income streams you should be creating.

CHAPTER FOUR

Membership Sites

Many websites now have an area that is protected by a membership-only portion. This is a very good idea as it means you can have free visitors that you can attract with an array of interesting and valued items and then suggest to them that they can get the full benefits of your site and save money by joining for a nominal fee. This can be a very powerful way to generate online income and operate a service-based business. If you have your members paying a monthly or yearly fee to get access to a password-protected area where exclusive content is made available and you offer exceptional value and a broad interest base (or a specialized niche) to keep your customers happy as well as wanting to spread your business by word of mouth to others (one of the most productive methods of building an online business), you can transform an average site into a very profitable recurring income-generating business, bringing a regular flow of income from the same customer base. One of the other benefits of a membership site is that you can start your site or launch it without it being totally complete. In fact, by only creating a small portion of your actual content, you can allow it to grow organically with content from your customers. This can be a huge benefit and you're getting paid in advance. This gives you the advantage of having a site that has content that people really want, you get quality, real time feedback, which helps you to provide and ensure that you are creating a product or service based site that is providing contents that your customers want, and not just a site that has stuff that you think or hope they might want. Often people will spend a lot of time, energy and money developing a fantastic site that nobody really wants and so nobody will pay for. The secrets of internet marketing are to provide relevant information that people want in an easy to find and understand format and at a realistic affordable price, but it must be user friendly and simple. The simpler the better as people will not bother if you complicate things. Selling Software

Selling software can be one of the most lucrative passive income streams you can try. Many people do not think of it because they do not have the experience or the technical skills such as programming, or the different types of software writing abilities, but this aspect is not important. The reason is because all of this can be done by other people who you can find on the web without much difficulty. Once you find a good program developer and have a good idea, (this is the important part), it becomes easy. If you can find a small, but very useful product or service in an area that needs to be addressed and offer a solution for what is needed, the software you develop does not have to be expensive or feature-rich to be successful. Often a small tool that solves a big need, if priced right, can be very profitable, getting back to those 3.5 billion people (plus an expected additional 3 billion over the next few years) on the net. If you can get $1 from 0.001% of those people you could be getting a return of $35,000 and If you can make that a recurring fee it becomes very profitable. Website Services Nowadays everyone is starting a website or webpage, whether it's using a home desktop PC, a laptop, or a hand held device, most people are not technically savvy. In fact, most are technically challenged. When setting up a website or page there are 101 things to do, including all kinds of setting up, programming, and small tricks to know if you want things to look perfect. Most people cannot be bothered and would be willing to pay someone to do it for them. If you have any talent at setting up websites and anything related to website creation such as SEO, post writing, creating graphics, creating website themes, programming, etc, then you could easily sell your services to people who want them. Places to find these people are Upwork, Freelancer, or some of the other virtual assistance sites. People also look on Facebook, eBay Craigslist, etc.

CHAPTER FIVE

Selling Instructional Products

At the moment, the fastest growing area on the internet, both for finding things and having an internet presence, is Instagram. It is so simple and effective it has taken over Facebook and YouTube because of the huge amount of garbage they have both now collected. Right now the biggest Instagram users are women over 45 years old and this is no joke. It used to be teenagers on Facebook, but because of the new smart phones, these often technically challenged users have become the biggest users and also the biggest spenders with an estimated user rate of 45%, and with their relatively large spending budget, these people are usually at the stage of life when they have a little spending power and are happy to use it. If you can write an eBook, then putting together an instructional or informational book or better still, some kind of eProduct such as a DVD series, software, app, instructional CD set, online course, podcasts, technical video or anything that would help people and solve any technical problems etc., this should not be too difficult (especially as you can outsource where needed). There is a huge readymade customer base on Instagram, (not that you should stop using all the other social media platforms as well), for this kind of product. These products can be sold anywhere and there is no interaction (unless you want it). They often start at several hundred dollars and can be updated as needed or you can ask for an email address to send them updates so these people become part of your email base. You should be trying to add to your email at every opportunity as it is your best source of high quality traffic. High quality in the sense that they have already purchased from you so are very likely to do so again, without too much persuasion, especially if you have provided good quality for money in the past. Revenue Sharing There are a lot of people who do not want to or cannot be bothered with setting up their own website and do not have a product to sell. This is where some of the revenue sharing sites can help provide you with the opportunity to earn money online without having to do all this extra stuff and take the time to learn how. If you wish to write for pleasure or as a hobby you can also make some extra passive income by writing high quality articles and submitting them to a variety of different locations on revenue sharing sites. Squidoo Squidoo is a writing platform that lets you create pages with rich content and then use those pages to sell products for profit and many people use it to market Amazon and eBay products, but to earn anything from ads on Squidoo, they need to incorporate a buying angle. Hubpages Hubpages is similar to Squidoo; it is a content community for writers. Members have their own sub-domain, where they post their content-rich articles (known as Hubs). As a writer for Hubpages (or Hubber), most of your earnings come from your own Google AdSense account and sites such as Kontera, as well as eBay and Amazon Affiliate programs. They use revenue splitting, which is done by alternating the code used in advertisements: Your code will be displayed 60% of the time, and HubPages‘ code 40%. This site is one of the 500 most visited US sites on the Internet. Infobarrel Infobarrel is a site that is smaller than Squidoo and Hubpages, but its earnings program allows you to keep a majority of the money that your articles earn often as a publisher and you are entitled to 75% of the revenue generated from the display ads on your articles. Infobarrel pays directly to writers, unlike Squidoo and Hubpages, so all you need is a PayPal account which can be an advantage if you are just starting out. InfoBarrel forums have a regular thread entitled 'InfoBarrel Earnings Reports', making it easy to see what other writers are earning.

CHAPTER SIX

Business passive income is a lie.

It's one of those myths that has been perpetuated for so long by so many experts we no longer question its validity... even though we should. After all, who wouldn't want an endless stream of cash flowing into their bank account without lifting a finger? That's the passive income promise, and it has wide appeal. Network marketing companies are built on this dream, seminar promoters have gotten rich selling it, and neophytes love the concept. In short, selling the passive income dream is big business. The only problem is... it's all a lie. Let's Put This Nonsense To Bed And Set The Record Straight... Unless the passive income comes from a truly passive investment source like a publicly traded stock, bond, or annuity, then there's no such thing as passive income. It doesn't exist except through passive investing. Take my ebooks as an example... In the get-rich-quick world of internet marketing, they would be considered passive income. I write it once, post it as available for download, and watch the cash roll in as people buy the book electronically and download it automatically. I never lift a finger, and the cash just flows into my bank account. Right? Well, not exactly... First, I have to spend months researching and writing the book. That's only after I have a valid product idea based on my extensive knowledge of my target market's needs, learned from years of directly working with them. Then I have to spend even more time learning all the technology necessary to create the book and implement the automated sales system. I have to invest in the cover, software, and monthly overhead to run the system. I also have to spend more time learning how to market the book, which involves implementing all the marketing tasks so people who need the solution contained within the book can find it. Then I have to answer customer inquiries when someone can't download the book, and answer questions from paying customers after they buy the book. Oh, and don't forget, I still have to account for my sales by maintaining proper records, filing the company tax return, getting a government business license, satisfying trademark requirements, recording the ISBN number, battling copyright violators, and about 30 other things I failed to list here. Hmmmm, that doesn't exactly sound like passive income to me. It sounds like a lot of work! The truth is I had to put in a ton of work up front before I ever made my first dime on an ebook, and I still have to run the business once the product is selling. The "experts" will argue with my example by claiming I could outsource the ebook research and writing to a virtual assistant in India or the Philippines. I could also outsource all the other work related to the ebook business and recline on a hammock sipping umbrella drinks while the cash rolls in. I've tried it and here's the problem: you either write it yourself or pay the price because you have to extensively edit a VA's writing. You either do the work or you pay the price in training, research, and management of the VA. It's all work in the end. There's no getting around it. One way or another, you pay the price. Again, there's no such thing as passive income unless it comes from a passive investment like dividend stocks, bonds, or annuities. Business passive income is a lie. Ebooks, membership sites, royalty income, and all the other models bantered about in the get-rich-quick / lifestyle-entrepreneur world are leveraged income models. They aren't passive income. Leveraged income models are characterized by taking risk and paying a large price up-front in terms of time and/or money with the hope of reaping disproportionately large rewards down the road. It's amortized income because you get paid down the road on an up-front investment. It's not passive income. Going back to my ebook example, I spent an extraordinary amount of time up-front researching and writing. I then spent more time marketing the ebooks to attract targeted buyers through the internet... before I ever made a dime. Buyers get the benefit of $50,000 worth of my time and highly edited, specific knowledge efficiently delivered for just a few dollars. (I've always said books are the greatest deal in financial education. Now you know why.) The only reason it makes business sense for me to do this is because my upfront efforts will produce an income stream for decades into the future with minimal ongoing effort.

In addition, they provide an affordable entry-level product that builds relationship and trust with potential clients for my more expensive products and services. However, it's not passive income. I'm leveraging my time and knowledge through information technology to deliver a long-term income stream that amortizes the massive price paid upfront before the first dollar is ever earned. It's hard work. That's how leveraged income works. It can be a good business model because it's scalable and offers many benefits, but it also involves various risks, an up-front investment of time and money, and plenty of good ol' fashioned work. The Final Nail In The Coffin Passive income implies something for nothing. Just sit back and watch the money roll in while you do nothing. After all, it's passive... isn't it? Sorry, no such beast exists in the business world, so get over it and don't waste the mental space on such nonsense. This isn't just a rant. It's important to get crystal clear on this issue because if you build your business model on a false premise, you'll get disappointing results. I help people design their wealth plans every week as part of my wealth coaching practice, and there's a right and wrong way to apply leveraged income.

CHAPTER SEVEN

101 Passive Income Ideas

1. Selling information products

Are you interested in selling information products online and tapping into one of the fastest growing online business trends in history? If so then get ready to discover how you can make money online simply by creating and selling information products on the internet.

In this article, you'll discover how to find a great market for digital information products, how to create a digital information product, and how you can market and sell your digital information products.

The Information Product Explosion

After the internet became a mainstream phenomenon in the late 1990s, it changed life as we know it. Communications, travel, music, government... shopping. Yes, retailers large and small have embraced the Internet as a way sell to customers across the country... and around the world.

E-commerce has grown exponentially over the last decade and shows no signs of slowing down. Consider that 40 percent of the world's internet users, that's more than 1 billion people, have shopped online at least once. And worldwide business-to-consumer online sales were $1.7 trillion in 2015... and that grew to $2.35 trillion at the end of 2016.

Large e-tailers like Amazon and eBay, as well as traditional retailers like Walmart, have embraced the online business model wholeheartedly. But even though they may dominate the industry, that doesn't mean there isn't room for small operators like you.

In fact, there's never been a better time to get involved in selling online as a solo entrepreneur. It's so much easier to make money with an online business than have a bricks-and-mortar store. The risk, the investment, and time spent are so much smaller.

Along with all this e-commerce activity has grown a whole new way to create and sell products. And it happens to be the easiest, most cost-effective, and oftentimes most profitable way to operate an online business. I'm talking about selling information products.

The Information Publishing and Marketing Industry

Before we dive into digital publishing specifically, let's take a step back and look at the information marketing and information publishing industry as a whole.

Though selling information products online is relatively new the industry is not. The idea of packaging knowledge, information, and expertise into a sellable product has been around for ages. When print publishing first appeared people would write "how-to" books, when audio cassette technology became available they would record their information in the form of audios, etc.

The idea of creating informative content and packaging it into something you can sell isn't new, but the idea of being able to do it online has opened up access to this industry to many more people and has made the opportunity much more accessible.

What Are Digital Information Products?

An information product can come in all sorts of formats, but at its heart, a product like this must pass on useful advice to the consumer. Despite the name, people don't want simply information. They crave tips and strategies for making their life better. They want guidance. And that's what the best information products provide, whether it's a video, an ebook, an audio, a webinar, a membership website...

Keep in mind that in this case, although a CD or DVD or a printed book is technically an information product, we want to focus solely on those products that are delivered electronically, usually via download or some secure membership website. For example, an ebook in PDF format, a video on a password-protected site, or an audio recording downloaded from your website.

The reason for this is because this way your customers can order products anytime day or night, from anywhere in the world, and get their product instantly, without you being involved in the transaction. It's money while you sleep. And because you are not physically printing or shipping anything; there is virtually not cost on your end.

Sure, you will have to handle customer service and keep an eye on sales. But it's much less hassle than having to keep track and send out orders.

Why You Should Sell Digital Information Products Online

There are several more advantages with digital information products.

They are easy and cheap to create. You can make a digital information product using nothing but your time and mental energy. That's free when it comes to your investment money-wise. You just need ideas. Then you write your ebook, film your video, record your audio, create your webinar... whatever you plan to do. This also means that if the product doesn't sell as well as you like, you haven't sunk any money into the project. That reduces your risk and financial exposure because you don't have to committ to creating physical products or purchasing and storing large amounts of inventory.

It's virtually free to store them. Because these products are digital, they are simply space on a server, on your computer (make sure to back it up), or on the cloud. For people with physical products, if they're not doing online drop shipping, they have to carry large inventories. That costs money to store and manage all that product if you have a warehouse and have hired a fulfillment house or other provider to oversee it. And don't even think about doing it at home — you'll quickly become overwhelmed. Much better to stick with digital in which your products take up basically no space. You can store large amounts of video, audio, and digital files online at very minimal expense to store and deliver those products to your end users.

At this point, you might be worried. You're thinking that if you have digital products being sent to customers... what's to stop them from sending copies to their friends or selling it on their own? Nothing really. But rest assured that 99.9 percent of your customers won't do this. And for the most part information marketers aren't too concerned about this issue cannibalizing sales.

Another way to look at this is even if someone did get access to one of your products without paying for it, they may love your stuff and become a true fan who purchases all your other products, services, etc.

How to Find a Profitable Market for Information Products

So how do create your own information products... and make sure they'll be bestsellers?

The first step is research. You need to follow the trends and figure out what the most profitable niche markets online are right now and what format would work best to meet that need. A great place to start is with your own interests. If you can match a profitable business with a passion, you're all set.

So start with an interest you have. Then start checking around online to see whether you are the only one who loves... online poker, for example. Look for blogs, Facebook groups, and online forums for discussions about this niche. Look at the mainstream news — is it mentioned? Look at retailers like Amazon or eBay to see what products they have for sale in this niche.

For information products in particular, you should check out the site Clickbank.com, which used to specialize in information products although it has branched out into other areas.

You'll find many categories in all of these places, from yoga to dog training to travel planning to weight loss and fitness... there's sure to be something that you're interested in.

From all these sources you'll get a good sense of whether or not this a viable trend with sales potential. You should also research what sorts of products are offered, the topics they cover, the prices... this is also vital market data you can use to guide as you create and sell your own similar information products. You're not plagiarizing or ripping off — you're getting inspiration.

It may seem counterintuitive to seek out thriving markets and then try to join in. But that simply means that there is a ready market for your products. It's not good to be a pioneer and try to create a market from scratch — that's often a recipe for failure. Your prospect's follow trends and latch on to fads... you should too. At least until the next trend comes along.

Once you've found a market that you are passionate about and is also profitable, it's time to actually create a product for this market.

How to Create Digital Information Products

As far as creating your information products, that's easy too. Remember that the content, whatever the format, should be useful advice. You could create how-to guides, strategies, tips, and tricks... provide something the prospect can't get on their own.

For ebooks, magazines, and similar products, you can create them in Microsoft Word or Google Docs and then save them as a PDF. For the cover, find a freelancer on a site like Fiverr.com to create a professional looking cover for you for very little money — as little as $5. This will give your product a very professional look and feel to it.

To film videos you can use your smartphone or a simple point-and-click camera. Once you have the "raw" movie file, you can use an intuitive video editing software like iMovie (if you have a Mac) or Windows Movie Maker to create your own cleanly edited video.

A very popular option for making videos is to create a PowerPoint or Keynote slide presentation then use a screen recording software to video your slides as you go through and narrate a presentation. You can also show your web browser or other software applications as well. This is great for people who are too shy to get in front of a camera but want to leverage the power of video. Popular software options include Camtasia and Screenflow.

Audios are simple too. Just use GarageBand (if you have a Mac) or the Sound Recorder app on Windows Media Player to record your voice. You will need a microphone. You can also simply use a voice recording app on your smartphone to record audios as well.

If you're worried that you're not an expert you can always outsource this information. There are two ways to do this.

First, you can hire a ghostwriter to write an ebook for you, you can interview others using something like Skype or GoToWebinar to help you create a product.

Second you could buy the rights to products that already exists and rebrand them as your own. These types of products are called private label rights products and you can take the orginal files and put your name on them, and make many additional changes or updates to them as you see fit. The key is you don't have to be an expert to create and publish information products.

How to Market Your Information Products

In many ways, no matter how far we've come when it comes to technology and online selling... the same principles of marketing and consumer psychology hold true. And that's definitely the case with your online venture.

The name of the game here is direct-response marketing. Back in the day, this was done with snail mail flyers, letters, magalogs, catalogs, and other printed material. Yes, so-called "junk mail." But they wouldn't send it out by the millions if it didn't work. These days this sort of content is sent out electronically. And it still works like a charm to get customers to open their wallets.

The good news is that you don't have to spend a ton of money when you engage in direct-response marketing online. Email marketing is a virtually free method to reach sell your products. And that will be the basis of your marketing efforts.

The basic idea is create a list of email subscribers. You send them both useful content — free valuable information related to your product/niche, as well as offers to buy products. Sending them the free content will speed up the process of them knowing, liking, and trusting you enough to buy your paid products. The novelty of buying stuff online wore off years ago and now people have a lot to choose from — you must give them a warm fuzzy feeling to be the one they buy from.

Yes, only a small percentage of people will actually respond. But that's how direct response works. You should have enough prospects coming in that even a small percentage of conversions will result in a profit.

To build an email list, you can employ a variety of methods.

Search Engine Optimization: In a nutshell, you use valuable content on your website or blog to catch the attention of Google and get listed high in the search results.

Paid ads: Whether you use Google's own pay-per-click ads or banner ads or run ads on a blog network, this can be a viable option, albeit expensive.

Social Media: Networks like Facebook are invaluable at reaching a targeted customer base these days.

So how do you take it to the next level? You tap into that small amount of people who buy your introductory product, also known as a front-end product. You contact those people differently than your normal subscribers.

Because they have bought something, they are more likely to buy similar products. So you offer them more in-depth, higher-priced products, known as "back end products." That's where the big money is. A back end product could be one-on-one coaching or an event, for example.

Putting It All Together

As you can see information products make for the perfect online business. They're digital, easy to create and deliver. And the profit margins are huge.

So next steps...

Find your niche – make sure it has bestselling potential.

Figure out which format works best for your niche: audio, video, ebook, etc.

Create your information product(s).

Create an email list and then market to that list.

Profit!

Types of information products include:

Ebooks.

Membership sites.

Webinars.

Cheat sheets.
Online courses.
Reports and analysis.
Templates and teardowns.
Live events.

2.Rental income

Thinking about purchasing an investment property? Real estate has produced many of the world's wealthiest people, so there are plenty of reasons to think that it is a sound investment. Experts agree, however, that as with any investment, it's better to be well-versed before diving in with hundreds of thousands of dollars. Here are the factors and challenges you should consider before buying your first rental property.

Investing in rental property can be lucrative, but it can come with many challenges.

Borrowers usually need to secure at least a 20% down payment for a rental property mortgage.

Being a landlord requires a broad array of skills, from understanding basic tenant law to fixing a leaky faucet.

Experts recommend having a financial cushion in case you don't rent out the property, or if the rental income doesn't cover the mortgage.

Being a landlord can be a good way to earn real estate income, but it's not easy or glamorous. In addition to choosing the right property, prepping the unit, and finding reliable tenants, there are always maintenance hassles and headaches.

Do you know your way around a toolbox? How are you at repairing drywall or unclogging a toilet? Sure, you could call somebody to do it for you or you could hire a property manager, but that will eat into your profits. Property owners who have one or two homes often do their own repairs to save money.

Of course, that changes as you add more properties to your portfolio. Lawrence Pereira, president of King Harbor Wealth Management in Redondo Beach, Calif., lives on the West Coast but owns properties on the East Coast. As someone who says he's not at all handy, he makes it work. How? "I put together a solid team of cleaners, handymen, and contractors," says Pereira.

Pay Down Personal Debt

Savvy investors might carry debt as part of their portfolio investment strategy, but the average person should avoid it. If you have student loans, unpaid medical bills, or children who will attend college soon, purchasing a rental property may not be the right move for now.

Pereira agrees that being cautious is key, saying, "It's not necessary to pay down debt if your return from your real estate is greater than the cost of debt. That is the calculation you need to make." Pereira suggests having a cash cushion. "Don't put yourself in a position where you lack the cash to make payments on your debt. Always have a margin of safety."

Secure a 20% (or Larger) Down Payment

Investment properties generally require a larger down payment than owner-occupied properties do; they have more stringent approval requirements. The 3% you may have put down on the home where you currently live isn't going to work for an investment property. You will need at least a 20% down payment, given that mortgage insurance isn't available on rental properties. You may, however, be able to obtain the down payment through bank financing, such as a personal loan.

Find the Right Location

The last thing you want is to be stuck with a rental property in an area that is declining rather than stable or picking up steam. A city or locale where the population is growing and a revitalization plan is underway represents a potential investment opportunity.

When choosing a profitable rental property, look for a location with low property taxes, a decent school district, and plenty of amenities, such as restaurants, coffee shops, shopping, trails, and parks. In addition, a neighborhood with a low crime rate, easy access to public transportation, and a growing job market may mean a larger pool of potential renters.

Should You Buy or Finance?

Is it better to buy with cash or to finance your investment property? That depends on your investing goals. Paying cash can help generate positive monthly cash flow. Take a rental property that costs $100,000 to buy. With rental income, taxes, depreciation, and income tax, the cash buyer could see $9,500 in annual earnings—or a 9.5% annual return on the $100,000 investment.

On the other hand, financing can get you a greater return. For example, say an investor puts down 20% on a house, with compounding at 4% on the mortgage. After taking out operating expenses and additional interest, the earnings add up to roughly $5,580 per year. Cash flow is lower for the investor, but a 27.9% annual return on the $20,000 investment is much higher than the 9.5% earned by the cash buyer.

How to Get a Mortgage for Rental Property

Though a rental property mortgage is basically the same as a primary residence mortgage, there are some key differences. For starters, there are higher rates of default on rental property loans because borrowers facing financial troubles tend to focus on a primary home's mortgage first. The added risk means lenders typically charge higher interest rates on rental properties.

Then there are the underwriting standards, which tend to be more strict for rental properties. In general, mortgage lenders focus on the borrower's credit score, down payment, and debt-to-income ratio. The same factors apply to rental property mortgages, but the borrower will likely be held to more stringent credit score and DTI thresholds—and a higher minimum down payment. Additionally, the lender may take a closer look at the borrower's employment history and income and want to see prior experience as a landlord.

In general, here's what lenders require from borrowers to approve a rental property mortgage:

Credit score: A minimum score of 620, with better rates and terms offered with scores of 740 and higher.

Down payment: It's possible to put down as little as 3% on a conventional mortgage for a primary residence, but borrowers have to pay private mortgage insurance (PMI) if the down payment is less than 20%. PMI doesn't apply to rental property mortgages, so borrowers generally have to put down at least 15% to 20%.

Debt-to-income ratio (DTI): DTI represents the percentage of the borrower's monthly income that goes toward paying off debt. Though limits are more flexible for primary residence mortgages, borrowers should have a DTI that falls between 36% and 45% to qualify for a rental property mortgage.

Savings: In addition to showing a favorable debt-to-income ratio, borrowers should also have enough money in the bank to cover three to six months of mortgage payments, including principal, interest, taxes, and insurance.

Beware of High Interest Rates

The cost of borrowing money might be relatively cheap in 2021, but the interest rate on an investment property is generally higher than it is for a traditional mortgage. If you do decide to finance your purchase, you need a low mortgage payment that won't eat into your monthly profits too much.

Mortgage lending discrimination is illegal. If you think you've been discriminated against based on race, religion, sex, marital status, use of public assistance, national origin, disability, or age, there are steps you can take. One such step is to file a report to the Consumer Financial Protection Bureau or with the U.S. Department of Housing and Urban Development (HUD).12

Calculate Your Margins

Wall Street firms that buy distressed properties aim for returns of 5% to 7% because, among other expenses, they need to pay staff. Individuals should set a goal of a 10% return. Estimate maintenance costs at 1% of the property value annually. Other costs include homeowners insurance, possible homeowners association fees, property taxes, monthly expenses such as pest control, and landscaping, along with regular maintenance expenses for repairs.

Invest in Landlord Insurance

Protect your new investment: In addition to homeowners insurance, rental property owners should always purchase landlord insurance. This type of insurance generally covers property damage, lost rental income, and liability protection—in case a tenant or a visitor suffers an injury as a result of property maintenance issues.3

Keep in mind that standard homeowners insurance policies may not cover losses incurred while the home is rented out.4 Contact your insurance agent to make sure you are adequately insured.

To lower your costs, investigate whether an insurance provider will let you bundle landlord insurance with a homeowners insurance policy.

Factor in Unexpected Costs

It's not just maintenance and upkeep costs that will eat into your rental income. There's always the potential for an emergency to crop up—roof damage from a hurricane, for instance, or burst pipes that destroy a kitchen floor. Plan to set aside 20% to 30% of your rental income for these types of costs so you have a fund to pay for timely repairs.

Avoid a Fixer-Upper

It's tempting to look for the house that you can get at a bargain and flip into a rental property. However, if this is your first property, that's probably a bad idea. Unless you have a contractor who does quality work on the cheap—or you're skilled at large-scale home improvements—you likely would pay too much to renovate. Instead, look for a home that is priced below the market and needs only minor repairs.

Calculate Operating Expenses

Operating expenses on your new property will be between 35% and 80% of your gross operating income. If you charge $1,500 for rent and your expenses come in at $600 per month, you're at 40% for operating expenses. For an even easier calculation, use the 50% rule. If the rent you charge is $2,000 per month, expect to pay $1,000 in total expenses.

Determine Your Return

For every dollar that you invest, what is your return on that dollar? Stocks may offer a 7.5% cash-on-cash return, while bonds may pay 4.5%. A 6% return in your first year as a landlord is considered healthy, especially because that number should rise over time.

Buy a Low-Cost Home

The more expensive the home, the greater your ongoing expenses will be. Some experts recommend starting with a $150,000 to $200,000 home in an up-and-coming neighborhood. In addition, experts advise never to buy the nicest house for sale on the block—and ditto for the worst house on the block.

Is buying a condo a good investment?

Condos can be a good option for rental property buyers because they tend to be more affordable than comparable single-family homes, and they are often located in desirable locations (think: at the beach or a ski resort). Additionally, condos often have fewer maintenance demands because owners aren't responsible for taking care of the grounds or the building's exterior.

Still, financing a condo can be trickier than getting a mortgage for a single-family home. For instance, most lenders require that at least 50% of the units are owner-occupied and that the homeowners association is in good shape. It's also important to consider potential special assessments. You may be able to swing the monthly dues with no problems, but if the building needs, say, a new roof, you may owe a special one-time payment that could be thousands (or tens of thousands) of dollars.

Know Your Legal Obligations

Rental owners need to be familiar with the landlord-tenant laws in their state and locale.5 It's important to understand, for example, your tenants' rights and your obligations regarding security deposits, lease requirements, eviction rules, fair housing, and more in order to avoid legal hassles.

When to Hire a Property Manager

Rental property owners can manage the property themselves or hire a property manager. It can be a hard decision to make because property managers typically charge between 8% and 12% of collected rents, which can really eat into profits.

Still, hiring an experienced property manager can be well worth the cost. After all, it means less work and fewer headaches for you, as you take advantage of their industry expertise. In general, a property manager will:

Know how to market the property

Understand the local rental market and ensure you price the rental accordingly

Show the property to potential tenants (so you don't have to)

Screen tenants (for example, conduct credit checks and verify references)

Collect rent on your behalf and deposit the money into your bank account

Handle late rents and navigate the eviction process

Handle tenant complaints

Arrange maintenance and repair work

Pay property-related bills, such as property taxes, utilities, and insurance

To decide if hiring a property manager makes financial sense for you, ask yourself these questions:

Do I have time to manage the property myself? If you have another full-time job, you likely won't have the time or energy to manage a property on your own. This is especially true if you own multiple properties.

How close is the rental property to my home? Being far away from the rental takes more time out of your day and makes it more difficult to manage routine and urgent issues.

Am I willing to deal with tenants? Even if you do a good job of screening, it's likely you'll have to deal with unreasonable tenants, late rents, and evictions at some point. Is that something you're willing to do?

Is my rental property for short-term or long-term tenants? It might be easier to self-manage if you are looking for long-term renters. But if it's a short-term rental (for example, an Airbnb), you will be dealing with many different tenants—and potentially a lot of complaints and maintenance issues.

Do you need to be in control? If you will have a hard time handing over responsibilities such as choosing tenants and performing maintenance tasks, you may be better off managing the property yourself.

Weigh the Risks vs. the Rewards

In every financial decision, you must determine if the payoff is worth the potential risks involved. Does investing in real estate make sense for you?

Rewards

Because your income is passive, notwithstanding the initial investment and upkeep costs, you can earn money while putting most of your time and energy into your regular job.

If real estate values increase, your investment also will rise in value.

You can put real estate into a self-directed IRA (SDIRA).

Rental income is not included as part of your income that's subject to Social Security tax.

The interest you pay on an investment property loan is tax-deductible.

Short of another crisis, real estate values are generally more stable than the stock market.

Unlike investing in stocks or other financial products that you cannot see or touch, real estate is a tangible physical asset.

Risks

Although rental income is passive, tenants can be a pain to deal with unless you use a property management company.

If your adjusted gross income (AGI) is more than $200,000 (single) or $250,000 (married filing jointly), you may be subject to a 3.8% surtax on net investment income, including rental income.

Rental income may not cover your total mortgage payment.

Unlike stocks, you can't instantly sell real estate if the markets go sour or you need cash.

Entry and exit costs can be high.

If you don't have a tenant, you still need to pay all the expenses.

Should I Find a Real Estate Investing Partner?

If you would like to invest in a rental property but don't have the money (or expertise) to make it happen, you might want to consider a real estate partnership. In simple terms, an investing partner helps finance the deal in exchange for a share of the profits.

Keep in mind that a partnership isn't an "easy button," and it doesn't get you out of any work. You still have to do your homework, practice your pitch, and be ready to show prospective partners that the investment makes financial sense.

How Do I Find a Real Estate Investing Partner?

You don't need a Wall Street connection to find a real estate investor with which to partner. Instead, you can ask your own network of family and friends, find a local real estate investment club, consider real estate crowdfunding, or search for social media groups that target real estate investors.

How Much Down Payment Do You Need to Buy Investment Property?

Lenders typically have stricter guidelines when it comes to rental properties. Though you can buy a primary home with as little as 3% down, most borrowers need to put down 15% to 20% to buy a rental property. Rental property mortgages have a higher rate of default because borrowers in financial trouble tend to focus on their primary home's mortgage first.

Should I Invest in a Condo?

Condos are often cheaper than comparable single-family homes, and they have fewer maintenance requirements. However, it can be more difficult to finance a condo, and you must consider the ongoing association dues and the potential for expensive special assessments. When considering a condo for an investment, be sure to investigate the financial health of the homeowners association and the current condition of the overall building—not just the individual unit.

The Bottom Line

Be realistic in your expectations. As with any investment, rental property isn't going to produce a large monthly paycheck right away, and picking the wrong property could be a catastrophic mistake. Still, rental properties can be a lucrative way to invest in real estate. For your first rental property, consider working with an experienced partner. Or, rent out your own home for a period to test your proclivity for being a landlord.

3. Affiliate marketing

Affiliate marketing is an advertising model in which a company compensates third-party publishers to generate traffic or leads to the company's products and services. The third-party publishers are affiliates, and the commission fee incentivizes them to find ways to promote the company.

KEY TAKEAWAYS

Affiliate marketing is a marketing scheme in which a company compensates partners for business created from the affiliate's marketing tactics.

Digital marketing, analytics, and cookies have made affiliate marketing a billion-dollar industry.

Firms typically pay affiliates per sale and less frequently by clicks or impressions.

The three main types of affiliate marketing are unattached affiliate marketing, involved affiliate marketing, and related affiliate marketing.

Understanding Affiliate Marketing

The internet has increased the prominence of affiliate marketing. Amazon (AMZN) popularized the practice by creating an affiliate marketing program whereby websites and bloggers put links to the Amazon page for a reviewed or discussed product to receive advertising fees when a purchase is made. In this sense, affiliate marketing is essentially a pay-for-performance marketing program where the act of selling is outsourced across a vast network.

Affiliate marketing predates the Internet, but in the world of digital marketing, analytics, and cookies made it a billion-dollar industry. A company running an affiliate marketing program can track the links that bring in leads and, through internal analytics, see how many convert to sales.

An e-commerce merchant wanting to reach a wider base of internet users and shoppers may hire an affiliate. An affiliate could be the owner of multiple websites or email marketing lists; the more websites or email lists that an affiliate has, the wider its network. The hired affiliate then communicates and promotes the products offered on the e-commerce platform to their network. The affiliate does this by running banner ads, text ads, posting links on its websites, or sending emails to clientele. Firms use advertisements in the form of articles, videos, and images to draw an audience's attention to a service or product.

Visitors who click the ads or links are redirected to the e-commerce site. If they purchase the product or service, the e-commerce merchant credits the affiliate's account with the agreed-upon commission, which could be 5% to 10% of the sales price.

The goal of this model is to increase sales and create a win-win solution for both merchant and affiliate. The system is unique and profitable and becoming increasingly popular.

The internet and improving technologies are making the model easier to implement. Companies have improved how they track and pay commissions on qualified leads. Being better able to track leads and sales contributes to how they can improve or better position their products.

Those interested in pursuing affiliate marketing will benefit from understanding what's involved, as well as its advantages and disadvantages. Companies seeking affiliates will benefit from properly vetting and qualifying their partners. Overall, it is a low-cost, effective way of advertising products and services, increasing brand awareness, and expanding a consumer base.

Types of Affiliate Marketing

There are three main types of affiliate marketing: unattached affiliate marketing, related affiliate marketing, and involved affiliate marketing.

Unattached Affiliate Marketing: This is an advertising model in which the affiliate has no connection to the product or service they are promoting. They have no known related skills or expertise and do not serve as an authority on or make claims about its use. This is the most uninvolved form of affiliate marketing. The lack of attachment to the potential customer and product absolves the affiliate from the duty to recommend or advise.

Related Affiliate Marketing: As the name suggests, related affiliate marketing involves the promotion of products or services by an affiliate with some type of relationship to the offering. Generally, the connection is between the affiliate's niche and the product or service. The affiliate has enough influence and expertise to generate traffic, and their level of authority makes them a trusted source. The affiliate, however, makes no claims about the use of the product or service.

Involved Affiliate Marketing: This type of marketing establishes a deeper connection between the affiliate and the product or service they're promoting. They have used or currently use the product and are confident that their positive experiences can be shared by others. Their experiences are the advertisements, and they serve as trusted sources of information. On the other hand, because they're providing recommendations, their reputation may be compromised by any problems arising from the offering.

Advantages and Disadvantages of Affiliate Marketing

Affiliate marketing can yield great rewards for the advertising company and the affiliate marketer. The company benefits from low-cost advertising and the creative marketing efforts of its affiliates, and the affiliate benefits by earning additional income and incentives. The return on investment for affiliate marketing is high as the company only pays on traffic converted to sales. The cost of advertising, if any, is borne by the affiliate.

The advertising company sets the terms of an affiliate marketing program. Early on, companies largely paid the cost per click (traffic) or cost per mile (impressions) on banner advertisements. As technology evolved, the focus turned to commissions on actual sales or qualified leads. The early affiliate marketing programs were vulnerable to fraud because clicks could be generated by software, as could impressions.

Now, most affiliate programs have strict terms and conditions on how to generate leads. There are also certain banned methods, such as installing adware or spyware that redirect all search queries for a product to an affiliate's page. Some affiliate marketing programs go as far as to lay out how a product or service is to be discussed in the content before an affiliate link can be validated.

So an effective affiliate marketing program requires some forethought. The terms and conditions must be clearly spelled out, especially if the contract agreement pays for traffic rather than sales. The potential for fraud in affiliate marketing is possible.

Unscrupulous affiliates can squat on domain names with misspellings and get a commission for the redirect. They can populate online registration forms with fake or stolen information, and they can purchase AdWords on search terms the company already ranks high on, and so on. Even if the terms and conditions are clear, an affiliate marketing program requires that someone monitor affiliates and enforce rules.

In exchange, however, a company can access motivated, creative people, to help sell their products or services to the world.

Pros

Access to a broader market

Better accounting of qualified leads

Low-cost advertising

Cons

Subject to fraud

Less creative control

Vulnerable to theft

Examples of Affiliate Marketing

Amazon Affiliate Marketing

Amazon's affiliate marketing program, Amazon Associates, is one of the world's largest affiliate marketing programs.2 Creators, publishers, and bloggers sign up to have Amazon products and services shared on their websites or apps, and in return, receive compensation for the sales their sites generate.

Amazon sets strict criteria for the types of sites and apps that host its ads. For example, sites must not contain replicated content from another site or creator and be available to the public. Websites must be active with fresh content and suitable according to Amazon's standards. For example, they must not contain obscene or offensive content, promote violence or illegal acts, or contain any content deemed harmful to others.

Approval is contingent on a thorough review by Amazon staff and meeting a qualified sales quota (three within 180 days of the application). If an application is rejected, it will not be eligible for reconsideration. Once approved, commissions are earned as site visitors purchase products or services from Amazon.

Amazon Associates can earn up to 20% in commissions for qualified sales. Rates are fixed and based on product and program categories. As a bonus, Amazon offers special commissions on certain events.

Etsy Affiliate Marketing

Etsy (ETSY) — a global, online marketplace for vintage goods and other unique items—promotes its products through various channels, including affiliate marketing partners. To apply, applicants must submit an online application through its affiliate program portal. To qualify as an Etsy affiliate marketing partner, eligible candidates must be at least 18, have an active, unique website, have a brand identity, and meet other criteria.3

If approved, Etsy pays a commission to the affiliate for sales they procure—sales resulting from their site's promotion of the product. Commission rates vary and are paid on the order price. Etsy sellers can be affiliates, but they cannot earn commissions on their products without special permission. Etsy declares that it has the right to terminate an agreement at any time for any reason and that it can withhold compensation for any legitimate reason.

eBay Affiliate Marketing

eBay's Partner Network is eBay's affiliate marketing program that pays partners for sharing their personal listings outside of eBay Inc. (EBAY). The affiliate earns a commission and may earn credit towards their final merchant fees.4 eBay partners can also earn commissions on other sellers' items.

Commissions are earned when a buyer bids on or immediately purchases an item within 24 hours of clicking the eBay purchase link on the affiliate's site. For submitted bids, the commission is paid if the buyer wins the auction within 10 days of the bid.

Commission rates depend on the category of items sold and range from 1%-4%. No more than $550 will be paid on any one qualifying sale. Gift cards, items sold by charities, and special promotions are generally excluded as qualifying sales because of their low revenue streams.

Buzzfeed

Buzzfeed is a New York-based digital media company known for viral news and entertainment stories, quizzes, and product reviews. Its Buzzfeed Shopping segment features and reviews different partners' products and services. Visitors can read Buzzfeed's product reviews and select affiliate links to purchase. Buzzfeed earns a commission from each sale generated from its website.

How Do Affiliate Marketers Get Paid?

Affiliate marketers get paid a commission for referring customers to companies where they make purchases. These commissions can range from less than 1% to 20% or more, depending on the product and level of referral volume. For online campaigns, a customized link or referral code is used to track sales. In this sense, it is a source or passive income since the affiliate can continue to earn money once they have set up their campaign.

How Much Money Can You Make As an Affiliate Marketer?

Incomes for affiliate marketers vary, with some making a few hundred dollars and some making six figures. It depends on what is being marketed, how much influence the marketer has, the affiliate's reach, and how much time is invested in marketing products. Often, those spending more time marketing the company's products will earn more money.

Can Beginners Do Affiliate Marketing?

Becoming successful through affiliate marketing takes time, skill, and experience. However, it may suit beginners a bit better than alternative platforms since you do not have to invest in physical merchandise or inventory at the start.

Can You Start Affiliate Marketing With No Money?

Yes, there are several free platforms and affiliate networks available for little or no money. Instead, you will need to big a large online following through efforts such as blogging, social media posting, and so on.

How Do I Become an Affiliate Marketer?

To become an affiliate marketer, consider what platform you will use to promote products and/or services. Blogs are an effective channel for advertising and promoting as it allows the blogger, serving as an expert, to express an opinion about the offering.

After identifying a platform, find a specific category that you are comfortable with or interested in. A focused segment can better help you attract a dedicated consumer base. Research affiliate programs and choose one or more based on your needs, whether it be earning high commissions or generating more traffic. Lastly, develop solid and interesting content around the offerings and work to increase traffic to your site.

4. Invest in a highyield CD

A certificate of deposit (CD) is a product offered by banks and credit unions that provides an interest rate premium in exchange for the customer agreeing to leave a lump-sum deposit untouched for a predetermined period of time. Almost all consumer financial institutions offer CDs, although it's up to each bank which terms it wants to offer, how much higher the rate will be compared to the bank's savings and money market products, and what penalties it applies for early withdrawal.

Shopping around is crucial to finding the best CD rates because different financial institutions offer a surprisingly wide range. For example, your brick-and-mortar bank might pay a pittance on even long-term CDs, while an online bank or local credit union might pay three to five times the national average. Meanwhile, some of the best rates come from special promotions, occasionally with unusual durations such as 13 or 21 months, rather than the more common terms based on three, six, or 18 months or full-year increments.

Top-paying certificates of deposit (CDs) pay higher interest rates than the best savings and money market accounts in exchange for leaving the funds on deposit for a fixed period of time.

CDs are a safer and more conservative investment than stocks and bonds, offering lower opportunity for growth, but with a non-volatile, guaranteed rate of return.

Virtually every bank, credit union, and brokerage firm offers a menu of CD options.

The top nationally available CD rates are typically three to five times higher than the industry average for every term, so shopping around delivers significant gains.

Although you lock into a term of duration when you open a CD, there are options for exiting early should you encounter an emergency or change of plans.Opening a CD is very similar to opening any standard bank deposit account. The difference is what you're agreeing to when you sign on the dotted line (even if that signature is now digital). After you've shopped around and identified which CD(s) you'll open, completing the process will lock you into four things.

The interest rate: Locked rates are a positive thing because they provide a clear and predictable return on your deposit over a specific time period. The bank cannot later change the rate and therefore reduce your earnings. On the flip side, a fixed return may hurt you if rates later rise substantially and you've lost your opportunity to take advantage of higher-paying CDs.

The term: This is the length of time that you agree to leave your funds deposited to avoid any penalty (e.g., six-month CD, one-year CD, 18-month CD, etc.) The term ends on the maturity date, when your CD has fully matured and you can withdraw your funds penalty free.

The principal: With the exception of some specialty CDs, this is the amount that you agree to deposit when you open the CD.

The institution: The bank or credit union where you open your CD will determine aspects of the agreement, such as early withdrawal penalties (EWPs) and whether your CD will be automatically reinvested if you don't provide other instructions at the time of maturity.

Once your CD is established and funded, the bank or credit union will administer it like most other deposit accounts, with either monthly or quarterly statement periods, paper or electronic statements, and usually monthly or quarterly interest payments deposited to your CD balance, where the interest will compound.

Why Would I Open a CD?

Unlike most other investments, CDs offer fixed, safe—and generally federally insured—interest rates that can often be higher than the rates paid by many bank accounts. And CD rates are generally higher if you're willing to sock your money away for longer periods.

CDs have become a more attractive option for savers who want to earn more than most savings, checking, or money market accounts pay, but without taking on the risk or volatility of the market.

CDs vs. a Savings or Money Market Account

CDs are a special type of savings instrument. Like a savings or money market account, they provide a way to put money away for a specific savings goal—such as the down payment on a house, a new vehicle, or a big trip—or to park funds that you simply don't need for day-to-day expenses, all while earning a certain return on your balance.

But whereas savings and money market accounts allow you to vary your balance by making additional deposits, as well as up to six withdrawals per month, CDs require one initial deposit that stays in the account until it reaches its maturity date, whether that's six months or five years later. In return for giving up access to your funds, CDs generally pay higher interest rates than savings or money market accounts.

How Are CD Rates Determined?

Anyone who's been following interest rates or business news in general knows that the Federal Reserve Board's rate-setting actions loom large in terms of what savers can earn on their deposits.1 That's because the Fed's decisions can directly affect a bank's costs. Here's how it works.

Every six to eight weeks, the Fed's Federal Open Market Committee (FOMC) decides whether to raise, lower, or leave alone the federal funds rate.2 This rate represents the interest that banks pay to borrow money through the Fed.3 When Fed money is cheap (i.e., the federal funds rate is low), banks have less incentive to court deposits from consumers. But when the federal funds rate is moderate or high, banks can do better by paying consumers a competitive rate for their deposits.

In December 2008, the Fed reduced its rate to the lowest level possible of essentially zero as a stimulus to lift the U.S. economy out of the Great Recession. Even worse for savers was that it left rates anchored there for a full seven years.1 During that time, deposit rates of all kinds—savings, money market, and CDs—tanked.

Beginning in December 2015, however, the Fed began to gradually increase the federal funds rate in light of metrics showing growth and strength in the U.S. economy. As a result, the interest that banks were paying on deposits was rising, with the top CD rates an attractive option for certain cash investments. The federal funds rate began to fall in the latter half of 2019, then were dropped to between 0% and 0.25% in March 2020 in an emergency measure aimed at stifling the economic impact of the 2020 economic crisis.4 These lower rates currently make CDs a less attractive option for cash investors.1

When considering opening a CD or how long a term to choose, pay attention to the Fed's rate-setting movements and plans. Opening a long-term CD right before a Fed rate hike can hurt your future earnings, while expectations of decreasing rates can signal a good time to lock in a long-term rate.

Beyond the Fed's action, however, the situation of each financial institution is an additional determinant of how much interest it is willing to pay on specific CDs. For instance, if a bank's lending business is booming and an increasing amount in deposits is needed to fund those loans, then the bank may be more aggressive in trying to attract deposit customers. By contrast, an exceptionally large bank with more than sufficient deposit reserves may be less interested in growing its CD portfolio and therefore offer paltry certificate rates.

Are CDs Safe?

CDs are one of the safest savings or investment instruments available for two reasons:

First, their rate is fixed and guaranteed, so there is no risk that your CD's return will be reduced or even fluctuate. What you signed up for is what you'll get—it's in your deposit agreement with the bank or credit union.

Second, CD investments are protected by the same federal insurance that covers all deposit products. The Federal Deposit Insurance Corp. (FDIC) provides insurance for banks, and the National Credit Union Administration (NCUA) provides insurance for credit unions. When you open a CD with an FDIC- or NCUA-insured institution, up to $250,000 of your funds on deposit with that institution are protected by the U.S. government if that institution were to fail.56 Bank failures are exceptionally rare these days, but it's good to know that a bank failure wouldn't put your funds in jeopardy.7

The key to ensuring your funds are as safe as possible is to make sure that you choose an institution that carries FDIC or NCUA insurance (the vast majority do, but a small minority carry private insurance instead), and to avoid exceeding $250,000 in deposits in your name at any one institution.56 If you are holding more than that amount in deposits, you can maximize your coverage by spreading your funds across multiple institutions and/or more than one name (e.g., your spouse).

When Is Opening a CD a Good Idea?

CDs are useful in a few different situations. Perhaps you have cash that you don't need now but will want within the next few years—maybe for a special vacation or to buy a new home, car, or boat. For near-term uses like that, the stock market generally isn't considered a suitable investment, as you could lose money over that period of time.

Or maybe you simply want some portion of your savings invested very conservatively, or you shun the risk and volatility of the stock and bond markets altogether. Though CDs don't offer the growth potential of equity or debt investments, they also don't carry a risk of downturns. For money that you want to absolutely ensure will grow in value, even if modestly, CDs can fit the bill.

One of the downsides of CDs can also be a useful feature for some savers. For those who worry that they won't have the discipline to avoid tapping into their savings, the fixed term of a CD—and the associated penalty for early withdrawal—provide a deterrent to spending that regular savings and money market accounts do not.

One version of this is using CDs for your emergency fund. This allows you to ensure that you always have sufficient reserves on hand in case of an emergency because the amount in the CD will never decrease. And though you may incur a penalty if you have to dip into your funds early, the idea is that you would only do this in a true emergency, not for lesser but tempting reasons. All the while, you'll be earning a better return while the funds are invested than if you had deposited them in a savings or money market account.

Pros

Offers a higher rate than you can earn with a savings or money market account

Pays a guaranteed, predictable rate of return, avoiding the volatility and losses that are possible with stocks and bonds

Is federally insured if opened with an FDIC bank or NCUA credit union

Can help fend off spending temptations since withdrawing the funds early triggers a penalty

Cons

Cannot be liquidated before maturity without incurring an early withdrawal penalty

Typically earns less than stocks and bonds can over time

Earns a fixed rate of return regardless of whether interest rates rise during the term

Where Can I Get a CD?

Virtually every bank and credit union offers at least one CD, and most have a wide array of terms on offer. Thus, not only is your local brick-and-mortar bank an outlet, but so is every bank or credit union in your community, as well as every bank that accepts customers nationwide via the internet.

In addition, you can open CDs through your brokerage account. We'll explain more on these later, but in short, these are bank certificates as well. Your brokerage firm simply serves as a middleman.

Why It's Important to Shop Around

Before the internet, your CD choices were essentially limited to what you could find in your community. But with the explosion of online rate shopping, plus the proliferation of internet banks—and traditional banks opening online portals—the number of CDs that one can consider is astounding. It's now possible to shop for CDs at more than 150 banks that accept customers nationwide and allow for opening an account online or through the mail. In addition to that, you'll have access to a number of regional and state banks, as well as credit unions, that will do business with you based on your residency in their state.

Note that the range of CD rates across different institutions can vary widely. It's a mistake to just open a CD at the bank where you already have a checking relationship without investigating how its rates compare with those that you can earn elsewhere. You should shop for options available within your state or community, with several online tools able to filter these results and aid in your search.

The top-paying CDs in the country typically pay three to five times the national average rate, so doing your homework on the best options is a key determinant on how much you can earn.

How Much Do I Need to Open a CD?

Each bank and credit union establishes a minimum deposit required to open each CD on its menu. Sometimes a bank will set a minimum deposit policy across all CD terms it offers, while some will instead offer rate tiers, providing a higher annual percentage yield (APY) to those who meet higher minimum deposits.

In theory, having more funds available to deposit will earn you a higher return. But in practice, this doesn't always hold true. For instance, having $25,000 ready for deposit will occasionally enable you to open a CD that is not available to others with lesser amounts. But many of the top 10 rates in each CD term can be achieved with modest investments of just $500 or $1,000. And the vast majority of top rates are available to anyone with at least $10,000. A $25,000 deposit is only occasionally required for a top rate.

Which CD Term Should I Choose?

There are two important considerations when deciding what length of CD term is right for you.

The first centers on your plans for the money. If it's for a specific goal or project, the expected start of that project will help you determine your maximum CD term length. In contrast, if you're just socking away cash for which you don't have a specific purpose in mind, you may opt for a longer term to maximize your interest rate.

Second, you'll want to consider what's expected to happen with the Fed's rate. If it's anticipated that the Fed will raise rates—and bank and credit union CD rates will likely rise as well—then short- and mid-term CDs will make more sense than long-term CDs, since you won't want to be committed to a lesser rate for five years when new, higher rates appear. Conversely, an expectation that rates will decrease in the near term may trigger you to want long-term CDs, so you can lock in today's higher rates for years to come.

What Is a CD Ladder, and Why Should I Build One?

Smart CD investors have a specific tactic for hedging against rate changes over time and maximizing their returns. It's called a CD ladder, and it enables you to access the higher rates offered by five-year CD terms, but with the twist that a portion of your money becomes available every year rather than every five years. Here's how to do it.

At the outset, you take the amount of money that you want to invest in CDs and divide it by five. You then put one-fifth of the funds into a top-earning one-year CD, another fifth into a top two-year CD, another into a three-year CD, and so forth through a five-year CD. Let's say you have $25,000 available. That would give you five CDs of varying length, each with a value of $5,000.

Then, when the first CD matures in a year, you take the resulting funds and open a top-rate five-year CD. A year later, your initial two-year CD will mature, and you'll invest those funds into another five-year CD. You continue doing this every year with whichever CD is maturing until you end up with a portfolio of five CDs all earning five-year APYs, but with one of them maturing every 12 months, keeping your money a bit more accessible than if all of it were locked up for a full five years.

Some CD investors also do a shorter version of the CD ladder, utilizing six-month CDs at the bottom end of the ladder and two- or three-year CDs at the top. You thus would have funds becoming accessible twice a year instead of just once annually, but you would earn top rates available for two- to three-year CDs instead of five-year rates.

Why You Should Be Open to Odd-Term CDs

Whether you're building a CD ladder or are saving toward a specific goal with a known time line, stay open-minded to the very best CD deals you find rather than getting hung up on a specific term. This is important because when some banks and credit unions offer a promotional CD to attract new customers, they may stipulate an unconventional term.

For instance, some of the best CD rates you'll see have unlikely terms such as five months, 17 months, or 21 months. It may be to stand out, or perhaps to match the birthday that the bank is celebrating, or for any number of other reasons. But if you can be flexible in considering these odd-term CDs instead of the conventional term that you were planning, you can sometimes find yourself with a better-paying opportunity.

How Are CD Earnings Taxed?

When you hold a CD, the bank will apply interest to your account at regular intervals. This is usually done either monthly or quarterly and will show up on your statements as earned interest. Just like interest paid on a savings or money market account, it will accumulate and be reported to you in the new year as interest earned, so that you can report it as income when you file your tax return.8

Sometimes people get confused about this because they are not able to actually withdraw and use those interest earnings. Their expectation is that they will be taxed on the earnings when they withdraw the CD funds at maturity (or sooner if they cash out early). This is incorrect. For tax-reporting purposes, your CD earnings are taxed when the bank applies them to your account, regardless of when you withdraw your CD funds.8

What Happens to My CD at Maturity?

In the month or two leading up to your CD's maturity date, the bank or credit union will notify you of the impending end date. Its communication will also include instructions on how to tell them what to do with the maturing funds. Typically, they will offer you three options.

Roll over the CD into a new CD at that bank. Generally, it would be into a CD that most closely matches the term of your maturing CD. For example, if you have a 15-month certificate concluding, they would likely roll your balance into a new one-year CD.

Transfer the funds into another account at that bank. Options include a savings, checking, or money market account.

Withdraw the proceeds. They can be transferred to an external bank account or mailed to you as a paper check.

In any case, the communication to you will stipulate a deadline for you to provide instructions, with an indication of what the institution will do in lieu of receiving your guidance. In many cases, its default move will be to roll your proceeds into a new CD.

Missing the bank's deadline for instructing it on how to handle the proceeds of your maturing CD can lead to involuntarily locking yourself into a subpar rate for years to come, or incurring an unwanted—and potentially hefty—early withdrawal penalty because you waited too long before extracting your funds.

Should I Let My CD Roll Over?

As a general rule, letting your CD roll over into a similar CD term at the same institution is almost always unwise. If you still don't need the cash and are interested in starting a new CD, rolling it over is certainly the path of least resistance. But it's also virtually never the path of maximum return.

As we've mentioned, shopping around is imperative if you want to earn the top rate on your CD investments. And the odds are low that the bank where your CD is maturing is currently a top-rate provider among the hundreds of banks and credit unions from which you can choose a CD. It's possible that you'll do well with a rolled-over CD, but the probabilities are against you, and shopping around is always your better bet.

Even if you find that your existing bank is indeed a top contender, you'll be able to move into that CD purposefully and with confidence that you've done your homework to score the best possible return.

What If I Need to Withdraw My Money Early?

Even though opening a CD involves agreeing to keep the funds on deposit without withdrawals for the duration of the term, that doesn't mean you lack options if your plans need to change. Whether you encounter an emergency or a change in your financial situation—or you simply feel that you can use the money more usefully or lucratively elsewhere—all banks and credit unions have stipulated terms for how to cash your CD out early.

The exit won't be free, of course. The most common way that financial institutions accommodate a premature termination is by assessing an early withdrawal penalty (EWP) on the proceeds before your funds are distributed, according to specific terms and calculations that were set out in your deposit agreement when you first opened the certificate. This means that you can know before you agree to the CD if the EWP is acceptable to you.

Most typically, the EWP is charged as a number of months' interest, with a greater number of months for longer CD terms and fewer months for shorter CDs. For instance, a bank's policy might be to deduct three months' interest for all CDs with terms up to 12 months, six months' interest for those with terms up to three years, and a full year's worth of interest for its long-term CDs. These are just examples, of course—every bank and credit union sets its own EWP, so it's important to compare EWP policies whenever you are deciding between two similar CDs.

It's especially wise to watch out for EWPs that can eat into your principal. The typical EWP policy described above will only cause you to earn less than you would have if you had kept the CD to maturity. You will generally still have earnings, as the EWP will usually only eat up a portion of your earned interest. But some particularly onerous penalties exist in the marketplace, where a flat-percentage penalty is applied. Since this percentage can outweigh what you've earned on a CD that you haven't kept very long, you could find yourself collecting less in proceeds than you invested. As a result, these EWP types are best avoided.

Always check a bank's EWP policy before committing to a CD. If it's especially aggressive—or if you can find another CD with a similar rate and a milder term—then you'll be wise to stay away from the toughest penalties.

Specialty CDs: Bump-Up, Add-On, No-Penalty, Jumbo, and IRA

The most common CD type follows the standard formula of depositing your funds, letting them sit untouched until the end of the term, and withdrawing them upon maturity. But banks and credit unions also offer a variety of specialty certificates with different structures and rules.

Bump-up CDs

These are sometimes called raise-your-rate certificates. Bump-up CDs offer savers a chance to access a higher rate usually once during their term. So if you open a five-year certificate and rates rise during that period, you'll have one opportunity to lock in at a higher rate currently offered by the bank, which will then apply for the duration of your term. Occasionally, bump-up CDs will allow two rate increases, although only for long-term CDs.

Add-on CDs

Add-on CDs let you play around with your deposit amount instead of your interest rate. You can open the CD with one amount but make additional deposits to increase your invested principal. Some banks will allow as many add-ons as you like; others will stipulate a certain number of allowable add-ons per time period (e.g., per month or quarter); and a few will limit the add-ons to just one or two during the full term.

No-penalty CDs

These sound enticing, as they seem to provide the interest rate benefit of a CD, but with less risk if you need to cash out early. No-penalty CDs can indeed bridge the gap between a fully accessible savings account and a CD with an early withdrawal penalty. But as you can guess, "no penalty" comes with a price tag: a lower interest rate than you would be able to earn with a traditional CD. So it's important to compare the rates of no-penalty CDs with what you can earn from a top savings or money market account.

Jumbo CDs

This is another product you may encounter when shopping for CDs. Jumbo CDs are simply CDs with a large minimum deposit. No governing body prescribes the floor for calling a CD a "jumbo," so each bank decides for itself. The most typical threshold is a $50,000 minimum deposit. Some institutions call $25,000 CDs a jumbo (or perhaps "mini-jumbo") certificate, while others reserve the jumbo label for CDs of at least $100,000.

IRA CDs

CDs can also be a useful savings vehicle for retirement funds. Many banks and credit unions offer IRA CDs. Some have a separate menu of CDs that are available as individual retirement accounts (IRAs), while other institutions allow any of their standard CDs to be set up as IRA CDs. One difference, in either case, is that IRA CDs must be held in an officially designated IRA.

Getting a CD: Direct vs. Brokered CDs

If you have a brokerage account, you may have noticed CDs offered there and wondered how they differ from CDs opened directly with a bank or credit union.

The first point is that brokered CDs are bank CDs, with the brokerage firm serving as a process-simplifying middleman. That said, there are some important differences.

Lower Rates

Although brokered CDs occasionally offer rates competitive with direct bank certificates, the rates on brokered CDs are typically lower. If maximizing your CD returns is a priority, you'll generally be better off going straight to the source.

But what brokered CDs give up in rates, they counter with convenience, especially for those holding multiple CDs. That's because brokered CDs will be included on the same regular monthly or quarterly statements that you already get for your brokerage account, with all maturity dates and terms shown. This makes tracking what you hold, and when each will mature, much simpler.

More Convenience...

Opening a brokered CD is also a bit easier. As you already have an account with the brokerage firm, it will acquire the CD on your behalf. This spares you the bank paperwork of directly opening a CD and the extra statements you get afterward. Termination is also simplified: When the CD matures, the funds will typically move into your cash account at the brokerage firm.

...Unless You Need to Withdraw Early

Early withdrawals are treated much differently for brokered CDs than direct bank certificates. If you need to cash out a brokered CD early, you are required to sell it on the secondary market. Although access to this marketplace is provided by your brokerage firm and is generally simple to navigate, there are no guarantees on what price you'll be able to secure for your certificate. Key factors include whether you're selling during a rising or decreasing interest-rate environment and the time left on your certificate.

Selling on the secondary market is not necessarily a negative—it doesn't always lead to subpar returns. But what you give up is any guarantee or predictability on how much of your proceeds you'll retain.

Specialty CDs from Your Broker

Besides the standard brokered CD, there are two kinds of specialty CDs that are generally found only through brokerage firms:

Callable CDs

A callable CD is a specialized CD on which the issuing bank retains the right to recall the CD at any time. So while you hope to be locked into a certain interest rate for a certain number of years, the bank can decide at any time to end that arrangement and return your funds to you. This won't result in any penalties or losses for you, but it can cause you to lose the opportunity of a favorable rate that was locked in for the future. For this privilege, the bank generally pays a somewhat higher interest rate. If this is a risk that you want to avoid, then search your brokerage firm's listing for "non-callable CDs."

Zero-Coupon CDs

Another specialty CD that you might find at your brokerage firm is a zero-coupon CD. These CDs carry a face value, much like a savings bond does, and are sold for some lower initial price. The most important thing to know about zero-coupon CDs is that you will be taxed on the earned interest every year, even though you will not realize the certificate's gain until it matures.8 Therefore, careful tax planning is recommended.

How does a certificate of deposit (CD) work?

A certificate of deposit (CD) is a simple and popular savings vehicle offered by banks and credit unions. When a depositor purchases a CD, they agree to leave a certain amount of money on deposit at the bank for a certain period of time, such as one year. In exchange, the bank agrees to pay them a predetermined interest rate and guarantees the repayment of their principal at the end of the term. For instance, investing $1,000 in a one-year, 5% certificate would mean receiving $50 in interest over the course of one year, plus the $1,000 you initially invested.

Can you lose money on a CD?

Practically speaking, it is almost impossible to lose money on a CD for two reasons. First, they are guaranteed by the bank or credit union that offers them, meaning that they are legally required to pay you exactly the amount of interest and principal agreed upon. Second, they are generally also insured by the federal government, meaning that even if the bank or credit union went bankrupt, your principal would very likely still be repaid.59 For these reasons, CDs are considered one of the safest investments available.

What are the advantages and disadvantages of a CD?

Some savers like CDs because of the safety they provide, as well as the fact that they are perfectly predictable. On the other hand, CDs generally promise a very modest rate of return, particularly in recent years, when the federal funds rate is at historically low levels.1 If the interest rate offered is below the current inflation rate, then investors in CDs will actually lose money on their investment when it's measured on an inflation-adjusted basis. For this reason, yield-conscious investors might prefer investments that are riskier but offer higher potential returns.

5. Peer-to-peer lending

Peer-to-peer (P2P) lending enables individuals to obtain loans directly from other individuals, cutting out the financial institution as the middleman. Websites that facilitate P2P lending have greatly increased its adoption as an alternative method of financing.

P2P lending is also known as "social lending" or "crowd lending." It has only existed since 2005, but the crowd of competitors already includes Prosper, Lending Club, Upstart, and StreetShares.

Peer-to-peer (P2P) lending is a form of financial technology that allows people to lend or borrow money from one another without going through a bank.

P2P lending websites connect borrowers directly to investors. The site sets the rates and terms and enables the transactions.

P2P lenders are individual investors who want to get a better return on their cash savings than they would get from a bank savings account or certificate of deposit.

P2P borrowers seek an alternative to traditional banks or a lower interest rate.

The default rates for P2P loans are much higher than those in traditional finance.

6. Dividend stocks

Dividend stocks are companies that pay out regular dividends. Dividend stocks are usually well-established companies with a track record of distributing earnings back to shareholders.

7. Savings accounts

A savings account is an interest-bearing deposit account held at a bank or other financial institution. Though these accounts typically pay a modest interest rate, their safety and reliability make them a great option for parking cash you want available for short-term needs.

Because savings accounts pay interest while keep your funds easily accessible, they're a good option for emergency or short-term cash.

In exchange for the ease and liquidity that savings accounts offer, you'll earn a lower rate than that paid by more restrictive savings instruments and investments.

The amount you can withdraw from a savings account is generally unlimited.

The interest you earn on a savings account is considered taxable income.

Savings and other deposit accounts are important sources of funds that financial institutions use for loans. For that reason, you can find savings accounts at virtually every bank or credit union, whether they are traditional brick and mortar institutions or operate exclusively online. In addition, you can find savings accounts at some investment and brokerage firms.

Savings account interest rates vary. With the exception of promotions promising a fixed rate until a certain date, banks and credit unions might change their rates at any time. Typically, the more competitive the rate, the more likely it is to fluctuate.

8. REITs

Real estate investment trusts ("REITs") allow individuals to invest in large-scale, income-producing real estate. A REIT is a company that owns and typically operates income-producing real estate or related assets. These may include office buildings, shopping malls, apartments, hotels, resorts, self-storage facilities, warehouses, and mortgages or loans. Unlike other real estate companies, a REIT does not develop real estate properties to resell them. Instead, a REIT buys and develops properties primarily to operate them as part of its own investment portfolio.

Why would somebody invest in REITs?

REITs provide a way for individual investors to earn a share of the income produced through commercial real estate ownership – without actually having to go out and buy commercial real estate.

What types of REITs are there?

Many REITs are registered with the SEC and are publicly traded on a stock exchange. These are known as publicly traded REITs. Others may be registered with the SEC but are not publicly traded. These are known as non- traded REITs (also known as non-exchange traded REITs). This is one of the most important distinctions among the various kinds of REITs. Before investing in a REIT, you should understand whether or not it is publicly traded, and how this could affect the benefits and risks to you.

What are the benefits and risks of REITs?

REITs offer a way to include real estate in one's investment portfolio. Additionally, some REITs may offer higher dividend yields than some other investments.

But there are some risks, especially with non-exchange traded REITs. Because they do not trade on a stock exchange, non-traded REITs involve special risks:

Lack of Liquidity: Non-traded REITs are illiquid investments. They generally cannot be sold readily on the open market. If you need to sell an asset to raise money quickly, you may not be able to do so with shares of a non-traded REIT.

Share Value Transparency: While the market price of a publicly traded REIT is readily accessible, it can be difficult to determine the value of a share of a non-traded REIT. Non-traded REITs typically do not provide an estimate of their value per share until 18 months after their offering closes. This may be years after you have made your investment. As a result, for a significant time period you may be unable to assess the value of your non-traded REIT investment and its volatility.

Distributions May Be Paid from Offering Proceeds and Borrowings: Investors may be attracted to non-traded REITs by their relatively high dividend yields compared to those of publicly traded REITs. Unlike publicly traded REITs, however, non-traded REITs frequently pay distributions in excess of their funds from operations. To do so, they may use offering proceeds and borrowings. This practice, which is typically not used by publicly traded REITs, reduces the value of the shares and the cash available to the company to purchase additional assets.

Conflicts of Interest: Non-traded REITs typically have an external manager instead of their own employees. This can lead to potential conflicts of interests with shareholders. For example, the REIT may pay the external manager significant fees based on the amount of property acquisitions and assets under management. These fee incentives may not necessarily align with the interests of shareholders.

How to buy and sell REITs

You can invest in a publicly traded REIT, which is listed on a major stock exchange, by purchasing shares through a broker. You can purchase shares of a non-traded REIT through a broker that participates in the non-traded REIT's offering. You can also purchase shares in a REIT mutual fund or REIT exchange-traded fund.

Understanding fees and taxes

Publicly traded REITs can be purchased through a broker. Generally, you can purchase the common stock, preferred stock, or debt security of a publicly traded REIT. Brokerage fees will apply.

Non-traded REITs are typically sold by a broker or financial adviser. Non-traded REITs generally have high up-front fees. Sales commissions and upfront offering fees usually total approximately 9 to 10 percent of the investment. These costs lower the value of the investment by a significant amount.

Special Tax Considerations

Most REITS pay out at least 100 percent of their taxable income to their shareholders. The shareholders of a REIT are responsible for paying taxes on the dividends and any capital gains they receive in connection with their investment in the REIT. Dividends paid by REITs generally are treated as ordinary income and are not entitled to the reduced tax rates on other types of corporate dividends. Consider consulting your tax adviser before investing in REITs.

Avoiding fraud

Be wary of any person who attempts to sell REITs that are not registered with the SEC.

You can verify the registration of both publicly traded and non-traded REITs through the SEC's EDGAR system. You can also use EDGAR to review a REIT's annual and quarterly reports as well as any offering prospectus. For more on how to use EDGAR, please visit Research Public Companies.

You should also check out the broker or investment adviser who recommends purchasing a REIT. To learn how to do so, please visit Working with Brokers and Investment Advisers.

9. Rent out a room in your house

Most people think of landlords and tenants living in separate spaces, but what about when you decide to rent out a room in your home? When you do this, you become a landlord just as surely as if you owned another building that you would be renting out completely.

Still, the rules and regulations might be different when it comes to renting out rooms where you live versus renting out the complete property. To be a successful landlord, in either case, it is important that you learn the particulars. Without them, you could end up in legal trouble!

In the event that you decide you want to rent a room, many of the same lessons, tips, and procedures can be implemented to ensure that you and your tenant roommate are conducting business in a fair and legal way.

The information in today's guide will help you become a legal landlord at your own property with as little complication as possible all while you earn some extra cash.

If you have unused space in your home, renting out a room might be a nice way to earn some extra cash. Renting out a room in your house may be an actual bedroom, mother-in-law space, or some combination of bedroom and bathroom, plus kitchen access.

No matter what space you decide to rent, realize that it means you will have another person living in your home. There will be times when you get along wonderfully and also when they will probably get on your nerves at some point.

Remember that renting out a room is different from subletting, which happens when you are renting a place you don't own, but rent your space to someone else, while still being responsible for rent to the landlord.

Renting out a room in the property you own is a different situation, which is more of a landlord/tenant relationship than two renters together.

10. Advertise on your car

11. Pay Off Some Debt

Paying down your debt faster may help you get a head start on your goals, whether it's applying for new credit, saving on the cost of borrowing, or just reducing your debt. Here are some strategies to think about when considering repayment plans that could help you pay your debt off faster.

12. Refinance Your Mortgage

Refinancing a mortgage means paying off an existing loan and replacing it with a new one. There are many reasons why homeowners refinance:

To obtain a lower interest rate

To shorten the term of their mortgage

To convert from an adjustable-rate mortgage (ARM) to a fixed-rate mortgage, or vice versa

To tap into home equity to raise funds to deal with a financial emergency, finance a large purchase, or consolidate debt

Since refinancing can cost between 3% and 6% of a loan's principal and—as with an original mortgage—requires an appraisal, title search, and application fees, it's important for a homeowner to determine whether refinancing is a wise financial decision.

Getting a mortgage with a lower interest rate is one of the best reasons to refinance.

When interest rates drop, consider refinancing to shorten the term of your mortgage and pay significantly less in interest payments.

Switching to a fixed-rate mortgage—or to an adjustable-rate one—can make sense depending on the rates and how long you plan to remain in your current home.

Tapping equity or consolidating debt are other reasons to refinance—but beware, doing so can sometimes worsen debt problems.

13. Invest In A Business

Two ways you can invest in a small business are by lending capital to the business or buying company shares. By lending to a business or buying part of the company, you can earn a return in the form of interest, dividends or appreciation.Investing in a small business is a way investors can not only grow their portfolio but help local business owners on their journey to financial independence. It's a way to create, nurture, and grow an asset that can generate more than capital for an investor.

14. Sell an eBook Online

Everyone knows that a free ebook is one of the best lead magnet strategies for businesses of any size. But did you know there's a whole other ebook world where you can actually make money?

Even though free ebooks offer value to the subscriber exchanging their email for the download, paid-for ebooks must deliver a wealth of valuable information plus actionable advice for the reader.

Are you an expert at something with lots to share? Or are you a great storyteller? Either way, you can make money selling ebooks. All you need is — well — ebooks, and a good dose of productivity, effort and passion. If you feel like this is the right next step for your business, this guide is for you.

assive income is one of the most sought-after sources of income today. It means you're able to generate income with minimal labor involved. In other words, work less and earn more. Who doesn't want that, right?

Well, ebooks are a great addition to any passive income strategy. Why? Because once you create an ebook, market it and share it, it can technically sell itself.

Now, it takes a decent amount of effort to write valuable content. Not to mention, building a strong brand that will carry your ebook to success is not an overnight task.

But when you do set everything up correctly, ebooks can help you make money for a long time. In fact, the more evergreen your content is, and the more you keep promoting and updating it, the longer the life of your ebook.

15. Create a Course on Udemy

How to create an online course using Udemy's recommended course creation process

How to access and use tools and resources available to you as an Udemy instructor

Use the Marketplace Insights tool to identify in-demand topics to validate or refine your course topic

Learn how to define your ideal learners for your course

Determine and write clear learning objectives

Create practical activities and assessments to drive an engaging and high-quality course

Create a well-structured course outline

Produce your course content following best practices for recording and editing your videos

Write a compelling course landing page that attracts the right learners to your course

Launch your course successfully

Use your instructor dashboard to manage and evolve your course, and to grow your audience on Udemy

16. Selling Stock Photos

The ability to make money as a photographer, like a YouTuber or Instagrammer, is all about harnessing that same creativity at the heart of your work and applying it to the monetisation of your talents.

It can seem hard to make it when anyone with the newest iPhone can call themselves a "photographer" and everyone is using some sort of free photo editing software. But success, for most creators who turn to entrepreneurship, comes down to three things:

Finding your niche

Building an audience

Creating several streams of income

This guide will explore some of the things you should know about selling photos online with resources and business ideas to help you make your photography-based business a reality.

How to sell photos online: Two essential steps

1. Define your niche

Every successful photographer has a consistent style or theme that runs through their work. Whether your thing is travel, fashion, cityscapes, nature, food, etc., consistency is key.

People follow other people online to see more of whatever it is that interested them in the first place. People unfollow other people when those expectations aren't met.

Finding your niche if you want to sell pictures online is typically something you feel your way into as you see which styles and photos resonate with your audience. But you can also evaluate the demand for certain topics using keyword research to analyse the search volume for terms related to your photographs.

Keywords Everywhere is a browser extension that shows you the search volume right below your Google search, making it easy to find and experiment with in-demand subjects and angles to see what you can cater to with your photographs.

17. Licensing Music

Music licensing is the licensed use of copyrighted music. Music licensing is intended to ensure that the owners of copyrights on musical works are compensated for certain uses of their work. A purchaser has limited rights to use the work without a separate agreement.

18. Create an App

How to make an app for beginners in 10 steps

Generate an app idea
Do competitive market research
Write out the features for your app
Make design mockups of your app
Create your app's graphic design
Put together an app marketing plan
Build the app with one of these options
Submit your app to the App Store
Market your app for maximum exposure
Improve your app with user feedback

19. Affiliate Marketing

20. Network Marketing

Network marketing is a business model that depends on person-to-person sales by independent representatives, often working from home. A network marketing business may require you to build a network of business partners or salespeople to assist with lead generation and closing sales.

There are many reputable network marketing operations, but some have been denounced as pyramid schemes. The latter may focus less on sales to consumers than on recruitment of salespeople who may be required to pay upfront for expensive starter kits.

Network marketing appeals to people with high energy and strong sales skills, who can build a profitable business with a modest investment.

A network marketing business can be a single-tier program, whereby you sell the products, or multi-tier, where you also recruit additional salespeople.

Beware of network marketing companies that create many tiers of salespeople or require you to purchase expensive products or training material up-front, Make sure to thoroughly research the company before you join.

Network marketing is known by a variety of names, including multilevel marketing (MLM), cellular marketing, affiliate marketing, consumer-direct marketing, referral marketing, or home-based business franchising.

Companies that follow the network marketing model often create tiers of salespeople—that is, salespeople are encouraged to recruit their own networks of salespeople. The creators of a new tier (or "upline") earn commission on their own sales and on sales made by the people in the tier they created (the "downline"). In time, a new tier can sprout yet another tier, which contributes more commission to the person in the top tier as well as the middle tier.

21. Design T-Shirts

Custom Ink's best-in-class Design Lab makes it fun and easy to create a great custom t-shirt design. Our lab offers tons of great clipart and fonts, and you can easily upload a logo to your t-shirt. Plus, no matter where you are in the design process, whether just starting out or in need of a second opinion, our experts are ready to help seven days a week.

22. Sell Digital Files on Etsy

Etsy is a great platform to sell your digital downloads because they can handle the delivery of the products for you. Once you created the product, you can upload the file to Etsy when you create a product listing. You can upload many files type including PDF, JPG and zip, with a 20mb file size limit for each file.

23. List Your Place on Airbnb

Step 1: Open your browser and visit the official website, Airbnb.com. Step 2: After that select Host. Step 3: Now select Add a new listing. Step 4: After that, you'll be asked a series of questions about your place, one of which is "Do you host on Airbnb as part of a company?"

24. Rent Out Your Car

If a car gets damaged while in your possession, then you will have to pay for the repairs out of your own pocket.

25. Vending Machines

26. Storage Rentals

27. Cashback Rewards Cards

28. Cashback Sites

29. Get Paid to Have An App On Your Phone

30. Save Up To 30% On Your Electric Bill

31. Start a Blog

32. Sell Digital Products

33. Store People's Stuff

34. Rent Out Useful Items

35. Fixing & Renting Property

36. Income Through Cash Back Websites

37. Drop-Shipping

38. Become a Social Media Influencer

39. Transcription

40. Start a Podcast

41. Become a Social Media Manager

42. Start an ecommerce business

43. Crowdfunded Rental Properties

44. Refinance Student Loans

45. Make Money Watching TV

46. Buy and Sell Domain Names for Websites

47. Create Software

48. Invest in a Food Truck

49. Rent Out Old Baby Gear

50. Sell Retargeting Advertisements

51. Freelance Graphic Design

52. Sell Your Clothes

53. Sell Your Plasma

54. Start an Etsy Store

55. Participate in a Sleep Study

56. Become a Notary

57. Customer Interviews

58. Become a Brand Ambassador

59. House Sitting 60. Consulting

61. Lose Weight

62. Participate in Scientific Studies

63. Design Logos

64. Be an Extra in Movies

65. Email Marketing

66. Create an Audiobook

67. Refinance Your Mortgage

68. Buying bonds and/or CDs

69. Building a niche affiliate website

70. Subleasing to roommates

71. Installing moneysaving apps

72. Earning credit card rewards

73. Renting out your tools

74. Get cash back for online shopping

75. Buy a blog

76. Produce an audiobook

77. Build a sales funnel

78. Develop a smartphone app

79. Generate royalties from jingles or audio tracks

80. Make YouTube video tutorials

81. Sell professional photos online

82. Build niche or "guide" websites for lead or referral income

83. Alexa Skills

84. Sell Your Music

85. Write a Guide

86. Create an Audio Book

87. Use Rewards and Points Cards

88. Cash Back Cards

89. Rent Your House

90. Rent Your Parking Space

91. Investing in coins and collectibles

92. Sell your coins and collectibles

93. Sell items on eBay

94. Investing in real estate

95. Software as a Service

96. Digital Downloads and Templates

97. Amazon Affiliate Marketing

98. Amazon FBA

99. Hosting your own niche website

100. Freelancing 101. Answer Questions

9 798887 494982

Printed by Libri Plureos GmbH in Hamburg,
Germany